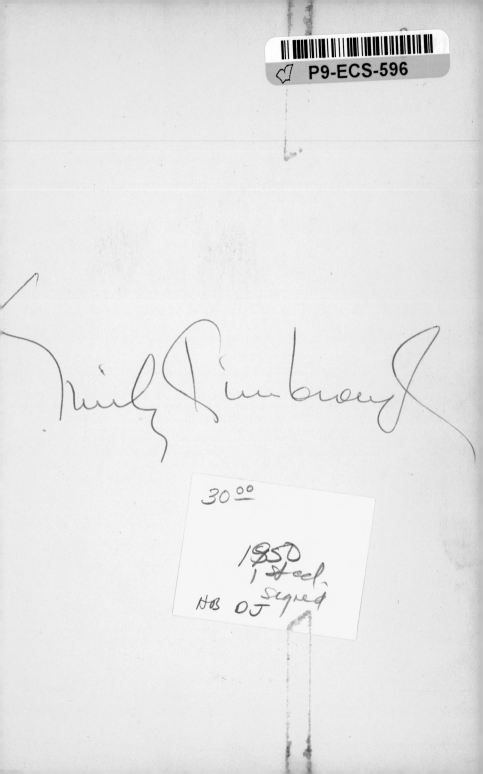

30 ⁰⁰

1950
1 tteel.
Signed

HB OJ

The Innocents

FROM INDIANA

Books by Emily Kimbrough

OUR HEARTS WERE YOUNG AND GAY
(with Cornelia Otis Skinner)

WE FOLLOWED OUR HEARTS TO HOLLYWOOD

HOW DEAR TO MY HEART

IT GIVES ME GREAT PLEASURE . . .

THE INNOCENTS FROM INDIANA

The Innocents

FROM INDIANA

by

EMILY KIMBROUGH

Drawings by Alice Harvey

HARPER & BROTHERS : NEW YORK

To Brother

WHO IS

CHARLES WILES KIMBROUGH

Acknowledgment

To Bower Kelly Thorpe for whose generous help
in recapturing and verifying memories
I am deeply grateful.

Contents

	PREFACE	xiii
1.	CHICAGO AND UNEEDA	1
2.	CITY EXCURSION	8
3.	FAMILY HOTEL	20
4.	OUR CLUB	35
5.	THE OTHER SIDE OF THE TRACKS	43
6.	VISITORS FROM HOME	58
7.	BROTHER'S SOCIAL LIFE	65
8.	BROTHER'S CULTURAL LIFE	81
9.	BROTHER'S FINANCIAL LIFE	96
10.	OPENING DAY	111
11.	OPEN SESAME	130
12.	MY FRIEND	140
13.	A RUSTIC AND A FAIRY	157
14.	CLOSE TO NATURE	173
15.	MARY GARDEN'S *Carmen*, AND BROTHER'S	189
16.	OUR WAVERLY	204
17.	GRADUATION	221

Preface

WHEN I WAS ELEVEN YEARS OLD, MY FAMILY MOVED from my birthplace, Muncie, Indiana, to Chicago. At the time, that was of interest only to our relatives and friends in Muncie. Today the incident as such is of interest to nobody. Therefore I should like to explain why I have had the temerity to tell it. The reason is that our family incident has happened to many thousands of families in this country. It does not occur to so many families in other countries. It is an American incident.

During the last few years I have gone each winter on a lecture tour, and I have read, in the local newspaper of nearly every small town I have visited, an announcement to the effect that Mr. and Mrs. Someone have moved, with their children, to Cleveland or Dallas, Portland, Chicago, Minneapolis, Washington, New York. Whenever I read these, I remembered how it was for us, when Mr. and Mrs. Kimbrough moved with their children from Muncie to Chicago.

Moving was an upheaval that changed, for all time, our way of living, our approach to society, our customs, even our manner of speech. The change was not accomplished painlessly, but it was permanent. When we returned to Muncie to visit, we were different from our family and friends there, different from the people we had been when we lived among them.

I have tried to tell the story of this gradual difference. I have not been accurate about chronology. I have telescoped time and episodes because I am not writing a diary. I am only saying to those who have moved from the Muncies to the Chicagos,

"Is this something of how it was for you?"

E. K.

The Innocents

FROM INDIANA

1. Chicago and Uneeda

WE WERE AT CORNWALL ON THE HUDSON WHEN MOTHER told me the news that our family was going to move to Chicago to live. We had a cottage for the summer in Cornwall, but Muncie, Indiana, was home. We were sharing the cottage with Mother's sister, my Aunt Lulie Robbins, and her son, Charles, my cousin, who was four years older than I. I was ten; my brother Charles was four. The fact that my brother's name was also Charles did not cause any confusion because he was always called Brother by everybody. Charles Robbins' father was dead, and Aunt Lulie taught at Teachers College, Columbia University. She had found out about the cottage because some other Columbia professors went to Cornwall.

Father had made the trip from Muncie with us and stayed on for two weeks, possibly in order to recover sufficient strength to go home again. Brother and I had begun to be trainsick within five minutes of leaving Muncie and had continued almost without interruption, even giving evidence of our indisposition in the dining room of the Waldorf Hotel in New York during a stop-over there. On the *Mary Powell*, a boat that had taken us from New York up the Hudson to Cornwall, we had maintained our standard of travel and been boatsick. Arriving at last at the cottage, Father had given as his opinion for what it was worth, he said, that it would be a good plan to transfer his business to Cornwall and live there, at least until the children were grown—anything rather than move them again. However, he had gone back to Muncie, and there had been no other suggestion of moving until the day Mother said she wanted to talk to me.

At the time I had no idea that talking to me had anything to do with moving, though I felt that it boded no good tidings. When Mother said, "I want to speak to you, Emily," she meant that she was going to hold up for consideration, or worse, my shortcomings.

But that afternoon she said "talk," not "speak to," and added that she would walk with me to Mr. Brown's, the farmer's, to get blueberries. "Speaking to" sessions took place in her bedroom. I brooded over this distinction while I went to the kitchen for a basket in which to bring back the blueberries. What made the situation the more confusing was that I could think of no recent episode worth a "speaking to."

Two weeks earlier, on the Fourth of July, I had helped my cousin, Charles Robbins, put a Happy Hooligan giant firecracker in the path our tutor took when he came up to give us lessons. We had lain in Charles' tent and started the fuse at the moment we saw Mr. Sawyer, the tutor, leave his cottage at the foot of our hill. Charles had worked out a contraption with a battery—he was scientifically minded—so that we could set off the cracker from our tent, fifty yards away. But the timing hadn't been quite right; we'd had no chance actually to try it out. The explosion had come off too soon. Mr. Sawyer was so far away he'd only been startled. Mother and Aunt Lulie said that was probably the only

The water was piercing cold.

thing that had saved him. We didn't believe a Happy Hooligan could have killed anyone, just put him out of commission for a while. We felt, too, that the responsibility was as much our mothers' as ours. It had been their idea to engage him in the first place because, they'd said, having a Columbia professor so near us for the summer was a privilege we should enjoy at first hand. We hadn't enjoyed it, but if Mr. Sawyer hadn't suggested having lessons on the Fourth of July, we would not have resorted to the Happy Hooligan.

The incident, however, had been dealt with powerfully, not fifteen minutes after the explosion. Our mothers were not ones to delay action. Neither was my mother one to call up old scores for resettling. Therefore this talking to on the way to get blueberries was bound to be for something more recent. Since Charles' and my activities had been curtailed and supervised since the Fourth, I couldn't figure out when either of us had had the time or opportunity for anything amiss.

I brought a basket from the kitchen, and Mother and I started down the hill. She didn't talk all the way down, and this increased my uneasiness because not talking was unnatural for Mother. We waved to Mr. and Mrs. Sawyer sitting on their porch, and Mr. Sawyer called that he would see me next morning at ten, as usual. Mother said, after we'd passed them, how splendid it was that Mr. Sawyer didn't bear any resentment and was willing to continue teaching us as though nothing had happened. I would have been happy with enough resentment for him to discontinue teaching us, since this had been our purpose, but I didn't say so to Mother.

We crossed a meadow and came to a row of trees that fringed a brook. Mother suggested that we sit down there while she talked to me. It was coming now, whatever I'd done, and I asked quickly if I could take off my shoes and socks and dabble in the brook; I felt the need of a little activity. Mother said I could and that she would, too. We didn't just dabble our feet in the cold water; we waded in and around rocks, and stood in pools up to our knees. The water was piercing cold, the stones were slippery; we were having a wonderful time; I'd almost forgotten the

talking, when Mother said, "Now let's sit on that big stone—" she pointed to a flat rock in the sun—"and dry off while I talk to you."

As soon as we were on the rock, our legs in front of us, drying, she began again, "You're going to be eleven years old this fall. That's quite a big girl, big enough to have a say in family plans that affect you. This plan I'm going to tell you about will affect you very much, so I want you to think about it. How would you like to move to Chicago to live?"

"My goodness," I said. "May I take Uneeda?" Uneeda was my kitten that Mr. Brown had given me.

Mother lay back on the sunny rock and laughed and laughed. I saw, to my astonishment, that she was crying, too. I wasn't sure because I had never seen her cry, but there were tears on her face. She slid down the rock to the edge of the brook, cupped water in her hands, and splashed it over her face, again and again. Then she inched back up the rock to me and said,

"There, that's better."

She made an X with her two first fingers.

"Look, Emily. This represents a crossroads. You know, where two roads cross. Pretend we're standing in the middle, Father, Brother, you, and I. We have to decide which road to take. This," she wiggled one finger, "represents Muncie. This," she wiggled the other, "represents Chicago. If we stay on the Muncie one, it means living in the house where you and Brother were born, where everybody knows us. If we choose the Chicago one, we'll be in a city so big we'll be lost in it. But Father won't be in Grandfather's factory. He'll be his own boss. And we'll hear music and see wonderful pictures. You and Brother will go to splendid schools. Those things are called advantages. I hope it's a good name for them. Well, anyway, that's where we are. And you ask if you may take your cat. Come on, let's go to Mr. Brown's."

We put on our shoes and stockings, I picked up the basket, and we went on to the farmer's. Mother began talking the way she had always talked before when we went on walks—about the things we saw and a story or two.

I interrupted her.

"Are you going to tell Brother about Chicago?" I asked. She shook her head. "Four's a little too young. He wouldn't know what Chicago is." She laughed a little. "But you do—the place where cats go. Want to race to Mr. Brown's gate?"

We raced, and she beat me because I was preoccupied. In bed that night I tried to figure out what had gone wrong. On the rock I'd been someone Mother wanted to talk to, not "speak to," and then I'd said, "May I take Uneeda?"

I'd been a dub. That's what Charles Robbins was always saying to me, "You're such a dub."

The next morning after I'd fed Uneeda I carried her down to the farm and gave her back to Mr. Brown. We were going to move to Chicago, I told him, and asked if he'd ever heard of it.

"Chicago's a big city," I explained.

He said he'd heard of it.

"Be a considerable change for you, won't it?" he added.

"Oh, yes," I said, "it'll be a considerable change. You don't take cats there."

2. City Excursion

WE ARRIVED IN CHICAGO ONE AFTERNOON IN MARCH.
Father met us at the Englewood Station. The first
thing he said after he'd kissed us, was, "Look around you,
children. You're walking along in Chicago, and it's going
to be home."

Mother added that she couldn't believe we were really
there.

I couldn't believe that we were either. It seemed to me
we'd been getting ready for Chicago ever since the day we'd
come home to Muncie from Cornwall. Everybody in town
had been interested in our moving to a city. At McNaughton's dry goods store, and Mr. Vatet's, and Mr. Hummel's
Bakery, and the Sterling Cash Grocery, the clerks had asked
us about it every time Mother and I went in to buy something, and had urged me not to forget them. At school I'd
told Miss Richey that it hardly seemed to me worth while
to take up the study of Geography since we were moving to
Chicago, and I doubted very much if it was used there: the
city was so big we probably would never go outside it. The
other children had been spellbound, but Miss Richey had
felt I'd better dip into the subject just the same.

As we walked along the station platform, Father told

Mother that our rooms were waiting at the Del Prado Hotel and that he'd hired an automobile to take us there. They talked about how exhausted Mother was and that she didn't know what she would have done if our grandparents hadn't let Brother and me stay with them at the Big House the last week. Between the moving and the parties she would have caved in, she said, if the children hadn't been taken off her hands. I looked up at her to see if I could observe any signs of caving in and decided regretfully that the phenomenon had not taken place.

Father said he still was mortified about his own caving in. At the time they had called it shingles, and I had been agog to see him, hoping, with awful dread, that he would look something like Grandfather's red tiled roof. But he'd only been lying in bed at the Big House, where he could be taken care of while Mother went on with the packing, and said he had a rash on his stomach that he wouldn't let me see. He'd come from Chicago to help with the moving and had been put to bed instead. Mother had told some of her friends, in my hearing, that Father's contribution typified to her a man's idea of helping and that from the first she had regarded with a jaundiced eye his offer of assistance.

Brother sat down suddenly on the station platform and announced that he wanted to stay there to see the trains. Mother asked Father to carry him.

"He's been either fussing or in a morose silence all the way," she said. "I've been telling him about the Field Museum and the lake and playing in Jackson Park and on the Midway, but he says he likes his back yard."

Father picked him up, though Brother tried to push himself into the station platform. Father said any big boy, five years old like Brother, would think the most exciting thing that could happen to him would be to come to Chicago.

Brother's answer was, "I'm a big boy, five years old. I don't think it's exciting."

He wasn't so gloomy, though, when he was allowed to sit in the front seat of the car Father had hired. He began to talk to the driver about its engine. The driver called back to Father in the back seat, "Say, what is this boy of yours, a Steinmetz?"

Father tried, not very well, to look as if he weren't proud.

"Oh, no," he said, "just hipped on machinery, that's all."

I sat between Mother and Father on the back seat. Mother told him about the parties in Muncie that he'd missed. She described one that I would have thought she'd have been ashamed to mention. The Dante Class, a club she belonged to, had given a dinner, and with Father out of town they'd not allowed any men but had gone dressed in men's dress suits themselves. I'd seen Mother in that rig when she'd left and was ashamed even now, remembering the way she'd looked. They'd had their pictures taken, she told Father, sitting along the railing on the George Balls' front porch, where the party had been. "Houseboat on the Styx," they'd called it, Mother said. She added that probably those were the last parties she'd ever go to except when they went back to Muncie to visit.

Father leaned across me and squeezed her hand.

"It's not going to be that way at all, Girl," the name he always called her, short for "my girl" he'd explained when I asked him why. "The Del Prado's a family hotel. You'll meet lots of nice people there right away and be into the swing in no time."

"Have you met any?" she asked.

"Well, no," he said, "but I've been so busy, and then getting over the shingles, I haven't felt up to much until now. But with you here it will be different. We'll meet them. You won't have a minute to yourself. Reliable chambermaids to look after the children. You'll be such a gadabout you'll scarcely come in for meals."

In the lobby of the hotel, as Father was introducing his family to the manager and the desk clerk, Brother made a very loud noise and threw up. This brought about considerable confusion but no uncertainty about the cause. The noise Brother had made was a whoop, and he had whooping cough. We were very nearly put out of the hotel

at once, though we'd only been in it about ten minutes. When Mother almost cried, and said we had no other home to go to, the manager gave in. He made us promise, however, that we would keep to our rooms as much as possible. Mother and Father must use the service elevator, even when we were not with them. Brother and I must eat upstairs and be taken far away from the hotel to play.

Mother promised all these things. We were hustled around to the back entrance and taken up in the freight elevator. For six weeks we didn't see the lobby of the hotel, the dining room, or even the front porch. I caught whooping cough from Brother. And Mother certainly did not turn into a gadabout. Even when Brother and I were over the worst of whooping, the weather was so bad we couldn't go out. Father participated in the siege somewhat as he had helped in the moving. He'd never had whooping cough. He couldn't even sleep in the rooms we occupied. He had to have a single one on the other side of the hotel. I asked Mother one day if she regarded Father with a jaundiced eye. She said, "At the moment, yes."

They had dinner together in the dining room, late, after nearly all the other guests had left, in case the guests were nervous, Mother said, about being contaminated. For the same reason they didn't speak to anyone, or perhaps it was because no one spoke to them. I'd ask Mother every day if she had made a friend the night before, and she'd say, "No —still a pariah."

One day Father was suddenly called away on a business trip that lasted two weeks. After that Mother ate all her meals upstairs with us and only went out to take a walk at night when we were in bed.

Father came back one Sunday morning, and the weather turned hot and sunny that day. The doctor said we could go out and that he was going to tell the manager that, as of now, the quarantine was lifted. We were safe, we could go downstairs in the regular elevator. We were free.

Brother and I were wild with excitement. Father said that to celebrate he would take us to Jackson Park for a treat. We would leave Mother so that she could have a rest after what she'd been through. She agreed that to have her children out of sight and hearing would be the best treat she could ask and waved us off eagerly. At the last minute I had tried to stay. There seemed to me to be a possibility of Mother's caving in, and I didn't want to miss it. I didn't mention the reason I was holding back and finally

"Father, a policeman wishes to speak to you."

was persuaded not to be shy about going on my first excursion in this wonderful city.

We walked to Jackson Park. The distance was greater than Father had anticipated. Furthermore, we hadn't walked any distance at all in six weeks. My legs ached, I was hot, and I thought very little of Jackson Park. McCullough Park, in Muncie, had a caged bear in it, I pointed out. Brother balked after the first few minutes and had to be carried. I think this situation was responsible for Father's idea of renting a rowboat and taking us for a ride around the lagoon. Brother and I were in favor of the suggestion, and that seemed to relieve our parent.

We enjoyed the trip. Father showed us the Japanese buildings that had been at the Chicago World's Fair, he said, when the lagoon had been built, too. He showed us the Field Museum, the biggest building we'd ever seen. We wanted to go in it, but Father said that though there wasn't much choice between rowing and carrying Brother while he dragged me, at least he could sit while he rowed, so we'd row.

We came to a distant part of the lagoon that looked like a stream in the country. There were no buildings to be seen on the shore, nothing but grass, trees, and early wild flowers along the banks, even violets under the trees. I pointed them out and said I'd like to pick some. Father said he'd like a chance to rest; he wanted to take off his coat, he was sweating hard. He added that he was out of condition; and that another time we'd choose, for an excursion, riding in a vehicle that moved under its own steam instead of his. But it was his idea on this one that we take back the flowers to Mother.

When Brother and I had as many posies as we could hold in both hands, Father said we'd better start home. He'd only rented the boat for two hours, he told us, and didn't want to go over the time because he didn't think he'd brought along enough money to pay for it.

At the landing Father had a little difficulty maneuvering us to the special place the attendant indicated. We hit several other boats and splashed a good deal of water into ours; the attendant shouted directions and complaints. Father was so harassed he didn't realize that a policeman standing on the landing, also shouting "Hey," was shouting it at us. But after the policeman repeated it two or three times, I said, "Father, a policeman wants to speak to you."

Father said violently, "What?" and whirled around so suddenly that he swept his coat into the water and very nearly turned over the boat. Brother and I grabbed the sides to hold on. Father lunged for the coat and hauled it in by one sleeve. He put it, soaking wet, on the bottom. Then he looked at the policeman in a way I never cared to have him look at me and said, "Were you speaking to me, officer?"

"I was," the man answered. "I wanted to ask you just where you got those flowers."

Father said under his breath something that sounded like "My God." Aloud he answered, "Why, the children were just taking them back to their mother. Very wild back there." Father pointed in the direction from which we'd come. "Not near any gardens or buildings. Nothing wrong, I hope."

"It's all park property, as you ought to know," the policeman answered. "It's wrong to the tune of ten dollars' fine. And I ought to run you in."

At this horrifying threat I gave a yell of fright and of such volume that Father, twisted sideways to talk to the policeman, very nearly went overboard.

"Stop that noise," he roared at me.

The combination of my yell and Father's voice set off Brother, and he began to scream. I settled down to a steady sobbing. I couldn't possibly stop crying. We were headed for jail. We would never see Mother or anybody again. Between sobs I expressed these convictions to Father.

"Of course we're not going to jail," Father roared above our noise to Brother and me. He turned back to the policeman.

"You're perfectly right, officer," he said in a lower voice. "I don't know how I ever came to do such a stupid thing. Children, WILL you be quiet? The policeman's not going to take us anywhere." We subsided enough to hear what *was* going to happen. He spoke again to the officer. "But I'll have to ask you to go back with us to the Del Prado Hotel where we live. I've come away with only some change in my pocket."

"Well, of all the nerve," the policeman answered. He put his hands on his hips and stared down at us. "I've never heard the equal of that. Come along with *you*? Honest, I WILL run you in."

I let out a piercing scream at that, and my father slapped me. He had never done such a thing in my entire life and it paralyzed me into silence. Brother, by astonishment, was shut up, too.

Father spoke to the policeman. He told him everything: about our moving from Muncie, getting whooping cough, being cooped up for six weeks, his wife worn out and homesick, and he trying to make good in a new job. He wound up, "I just plain forgot about a city park. The only one we've got at home, McCullough, isn't much. The children pick flowers there and at the Fair Grounds any time they want. We're just country greenhorns, I guess."

The policeman nodded his head several times.

"You've had a bad time," he said, only he pronounced it "toime." "I haven't the heart to be hard on you. I'll walk to the hotel with ye. You'll not get off without payin' the ten dollars, though."

Father thanked him several times and promised that he certainly didn't want to get off without paying.

The policeman helped us out of the boat. Father gathered up his soggy coat, and we set off. Brother and I were grimy from climbing around on the banks when we'd picked the flowers; Brother's tears had streaked the dirt down his face, and he'd rubbed it in with his grubby hands when he'd wiped his eyes. I supposed that I looked just the same. We were still scared, the walk back was just as long as the trip out had been, and my astonishment at Father's slap had worn off. I began to cry again, and Brother followed. Father picked up Brother. He was holding his wet coat away from him in his other hand. I dragged along behind, clutching my flowers; the policeman walked beside Father. Father kept muttering to himself and the officer, things like, "The biggest fool in seven counties. Ought to have stayed where I belonged. A city's no place for jackasses."

The policeman said something like he was sure Father would feel better about it when he got used to a city. I didn't pay much attention. I was bawling.

That was the way we went through the front entrance of the Del Prado for the first time since our arrival from Muncie.

The people on the porch and in the lobby were interested in our group. Those around the desk were interested, too, and in Father's asking the clerk for ten dollars, though Father spoke his request in such a soft voice the clerk had to ask him twice what he'd said. Father was holding his coat at arm's length from him, and it made a sizable puddle on the stone floor.

He paid the policeman and thanked him for being so lenient. The policeman hoisted up his tunic, put the money in a pocket underneath, and pulled out a kind of notebook with a pencil slipped through it under a rubber hand. A number of people watched him open the notebook, place it on the desk, push up three pages with the rubber end of his pencil, put carbon paper between, lick his pencil, and finally write very carefully on the top page. Nobody spoke. When he had finished, he tore out an underneath page and handed it to Father.

"There's your receipt," he said.

Father took it, looked as if he were going to squeeze it into a ball and throw it down, but stopped, folded it into very tiny folds, not looking at any of the people around us, and put it in his trousers pocket.

When the policeman had lifted his tunic again and put back the notebook, he nodded to Father and said he'd be going. He hoped things would be better soon for the whole of us and added to the people around the desk and the clerk, "Pickin' flowers in the park. Can ye beat it?" He started for the door but paused to call back, "Don't be takin' any wooden nickels."

The people laughed. Father didn't. He said to us quickly that we'd better take the service elevator on account of his coat and the way we looked and would we please hurry. We straggled off down the length of the lobby toward the back of the hotel.

When we were in the elevator, Father asked the operator if he thought he could dry Father's coat down in the basement by the boiler. The operator said sure he could. Father also took the flowers from me—they were dead—and gave them to the operator to throw away. As we walked along the hall to our rooms, Father said he would consider it a favor if we did not mention to Mother any part of the outing on the lagoon, just tell her we had gone for a nice walk.

3. Family Hotel

THE DEL PRADO HOTEL WAS A BLOCK LONG AND CARRIED A wide veranda across its entire front. A line of rocking chairs at the veranda railing was in such close formation there was barely room to pass between any two of them. These chairs were occupied in fine weather, but not haphazardly, by the guests. Each chair, or series of chairs, was a claim staked out by an individual or a family and could be occupied only by the proprietors. Our family's concession was almost at the end of the line because we were newcomers.

The Del Prado was a family hotel. The families maintained fiercely their rights in the dining room as well as on the veranda. Tables were not casually come by; seniority and determination had won the favored sites near the door. Our table was at the far corner of the room, near the kitchen. Mother and Father deplored the location, and that bewildered me. I considered it the choice site because to reach it we had to walk the entire length of the center aisle. We couldn't avoid being seen by everyone in the room. I needed nothing more to make my life in a city seem to me a series of dazzling marches. In Muncie a parade, circus, Decoration Day, Uncle Tom's Cabin, passed only

once. I marched three times every day, into the dining room
and out again. And though I needed nothing more, I had it.
Brother was not allowed in the dining room. Children his
age had to eat apart from us in what was called, for some
reason, the Ordinary. For those who did not have nurses,
and Brother did not, there was an over-all supervisor. I
described to him, however, as frequently as he would allow
me, life in the large dining room.

When I was able to bring my focus from the glitter of our
mealtime parade to particular objects on our route, I
noticed one day a little girl about my age. She fitted exactly
my conception of the tone of our surroundings because she
seemed to me like someone out of a book. "The Little
Colonel" herself, I decided, because that was my current
favorite. She had very white skin, blue eyes, and dark curls
that were smooth and even around her shoulders. Her hair
was parted in the middle, and at each temple, just where
the curls began, there was a vein that showed blue. The
day I noticed the vein I promoted her from "The Little
Colonel" to someone of royal lineage. I had heard about
blue blood. I persuaded Mother to change places with me
at table, without saying why. From that seat I could watch
Her Highness. I was a bolter myself, but she ate daintily
and sparingly; most delicate of all, she made little pellets
from the inside of her roll or piece of bread and then ate
the pellets one by one.

The lady with her at every meal was her mother, I supposed, and the gentleman accompanying her at breakfast
and in the evening, her father. I was not interested in either
of these attendants, but one Sunday noon, as Mother and
Father and I came in for dinner, the lady got up from their
table and approached us. She introduced herself. Kelly, she
said, was her name, and Bower was her daughter, Bower

Kelly. Would Mother let me come and play with Bower that afternoon? Bower and I looked around our mothers at each other and smiled. I was friends with this member of the *haute monde*.

That afternoon we played for a while on the Midway. We had only to cross the driveway in front of the hotel to be on its wide green lawn and central, hollowed-out section, also lawn now, that had been a lagoon, Mrs. Kelly said, in the days of the Chicago World's Fair. I only knew that the banks were wonderful to run or to roll down. But Bower didn't care for running or rolling, so as soon as Mrs. Kelly said we could, we went upstairs to see Bower's toys. Mr. Kelly was in their sitting room, reading. He was plump and jolly. He kissed Bower when we came in. I made a note to call this custom to the attention of my parents. I thought it something a royal family might do, kiss their children just because they happened to come into the room—well worth emulating.

Bower's toys were beautiful and placed carefully, each in a special place. Bower said that they had moved to Chicago like us, from somewhere else, only they had come from New Orleans. Her father went back frequently on business, and he brought her at least one toy from every trip, plus a whole box of Tootsie Rolls. I had never before seen a greater quantity than one at a time, out of a machine when you put in a penny, but Mr. Kelly had found where they were made, and bought them by the boxful, because this was the only kind of candy Bower liked. She divided a box with me. "Royal generosity," I said to myself.

I examined everything in her bedroom, all the dresses in her closet, and her underwear in the bureau drawers. There were bags of sachet in the drawers. Her mother made most of her clothes, Bower said, and put up her hair in rags every night to make the even curls. The nearest thing to a sachet that I could claim was a box of Mennen's talcum powder, applied indiscriminately to Brother and me after a joint bath, and my mother could not make dresses. I'd heard her say that darning taxed her ability and her patience. My curls were straggly and Mother did not put them up. She pulled my hair off my forehead so tight that my eyebrows were chronically raised, tied a bow on top, made the curls around her finger with a wet brush, and the curls usually came out within a few minutes. I decided that our whole family would have to spruce up before Bower came to play with me. My decision was confirmed when I noticed the set of silver toilet pieces on the top of her bureau. I had an ivory brush, comb, and mirror. She had brush, comb, mirror, clothes brush, button hook, glove buttoner, shoehorn, nail file, and nail buffer, every one marked with her initials. They were placed in a straight line, graded to size. Bower said she always put the set that way herself, no one else was allowed to touch it, and she got the line even by measuring from the edge of the bureau to the bottom of each silver piece. Probably what royal families did on their bureaus, I estimated.

In bed that night, in the room we shared, I told Brother all about the Kelly furnishings. He asked if Bower had an electric train or a Meccano set and boasted that he'd been taken that afternoon to see the Illinois Central trains go by, had very nearly had a spanking, but had missed it. He considered his day more eventful than mine, and I finally hit him because I couldn't make him change his opinion.

Bower and I met again the next day, and from then on we played together every afternoon. She went to school in the morning at the Kenwood Institute School for Girls. I had lessons with Mother. My parents had decided not to enter me in school until the fall term because by the time I'd recovered from whooping cough there were only a few weeks remaining before summer vacation.

Brother had a short preliminary round with learning, but it was a failure from my parents' point of view. He was enrolled in a kindergarten that was part of the "School of Education," a preposterous name, Mother said, but it was an experimental branch of the Department of Education at the University of Chicago. The University was next door to the Del Prado, necessitating, therefore, Mother pointed out, only a brief and pleasant walk to take Brother and bring him home. But on the evening of his first day there I heard Mother tell Father that she'd asked Brother on the walk home what he had learned in kindergarten and that she had nearly fainted when he'd told her. I was in bed when this conversation took place, and Brother was asleep. I got up and tiptoed across the room, where I sat on the floor with my head against the door to the living room. By the time I'd got there without making any noise, Father was making a long, low whistle. Then he said, "That's about as pungent a list of words as I've heard."

I put away in my mind for future use the word "pungent." But while I was trying to figure out why words were pungent, and if pungent was something bad, Mother told Father that, though she hadn't missed their general idea, she didn't really know what the words meant. Did Father? He said yes, he did, but that he certainly hadn't known them at the age of five. It seemed to him precocious. If this was experimental education, he was not in sympathy with it. Furthermore, public school would provide as rich a vocabulary at no expense.

That was the gist of their conversation, as I heard it, and as soon as Mother and Father had gone to their bedroom, I

woke Brother up. I asked, as I shook him, what the words
were that he'd learned at kindergarten. At first he didn't
know what I was talking about, but when he'd wakened
a little more, he said he'd promised the boy who'd taught
them not to repeat them to any girl. I couldn't believe what
I was hearing. Six years younger than I and daring to say
such a thing to me. I contemplated killing him. I com-

promised by telling him that he was being taken out of
kindergarten for being precocious and that I wouldn't be
surprised, only delighted, if he went to jail for it.

He was taken out of kindergarten, and I played with him,
for want of anyone better, all morning on the Midway. He
did tell me some of the words, under pressure, but I thought
they were silly. Just what a baby *would* learn, I said. At
noon I would make it clear to him that he wasn't to tag
after me in the afternoon; I was through with him for the
day. I would then write a note to Bower. I wrote it at a desk

in the writing room, but I did not leave it in the Kelly's mailbox at the main desk. I put it back of the carpet on the riser on the fourth step from the top of the stairway at the third floor, a place Bower and I had selected. In the note I would make suggestions of possible activities for the afternoon. I almost always was the one who made the suggestions. Bower decided which ones could be carried out and how they could be accomplished. If my schemes were too grandiose, she whittled them down to practical proportions.

Bower introduced me to some of the other children in the hotel, and we approached together those she didn't know. The children came from all parts of the country. All of us called "home" the place from which we had moved. We knew very little of Chicago and were not interested in it. Our social life was in the hotel. Once a child left the hotel, that friend was lost to us, though the family may have moved only to an apartment a few blocks away. Our group admitted inexorably no one but a hotel dweller. Therefore we were wary of transients. The selected few included Pauline Foster, who had the longest and fastest legs; she could beat any of the boys in a race and was always challenging them; Esther Keane, who wore a wide ribbon band and large rosette around her curls; and Jean Cattell, whose hair was red. There were more boys than girls in the circle: Phil Bergstresser, whose name was Lawrence—he was called Phil because he came from Philadelphia; Stuffy Reber, Pauline especially wanted to race him; Richard Knott, very tall, thin, and blond; Ralph Shankland, tall and dark; and Walter Wicker, who was a good runner.

Our first enterprise as a group was the forming of a sample collecting and trading organization. We cut out from magazines advertisements that promised a sample of the product on the receipt of two to four cents' postage, and

Bower allotted to each of us the particular samples to be ordered so as to avoid duplication. They came in tins, boxes, jars, and bottles; they included powders, shaving lotions, candies, depilatories, mouth washes, et cetera; it was a rich field and ours for the asking. The arrival of these packages caused considerable excitement, but that was nothing to the tension of the trading post. We would gather in the afternoon on the lawn of the Midway in front of the hotel, each member bringing a large box that contained his samples. We would arrange these boxes like display cases and then move about from one to the other, swapping. Children were not encouraged to play in the lobby, no family had a sitting room large enough to accommodate all of us, so the Midway was our place of assembly except on bad days, when we were allowed to use the Ordinary. Outdoors we would trade as long as we could see. There was a man who came by on a bicycle to light, with a long rod and taper, the gas lamps along the Midway. He frequently stopped to referee an aggressive last swap or two in the dimming light.

Sometimes a guest in the hotel who owned a big red automobile would interrupt us to take the group for a ride around the park. We didn't know the driver's name, but our mothers had told us that he had lost all his family in the Iroquois fire and that he'd said he felt less lonely if he filled up his machine with children. We were always to go with him whenever he asked us. We agreed and permitted him to break into our trading only because we hoped, with happy dread, that the day would come when he would tell us about the fire. He never did, but one day as we were riding around the park, he told us about Halley's comet. We'd never see another comet in our lifetime, he said.

We discussed this among ourselves when he had deposited us back at the trading post. We'd heard some mention of it before, but none of us had been particularly interested. Now it was worth considering because of one thing our friend with the automobile had said—that you wouldn't be able to see it until around two-thirty in the morning. One of the boys pointed out, as we argued the importance of a comet, that fireworks were over by ten at the latest. This comet wouldn't even start until after two. When we broke up at dusk that evening, we had decided that under the circumstances the phenomenon was worth our consideration. Reflecting on this decision that night in bed, I pictured how it could be fun if we all saw it together but dull if each of us looked at it only with our parents.

Next day I pointed out to Bower this gap between pleasure and boredom. She agreed with me but felt that there were practical obstacles to our enjoying the comet as a group. How would we assemble at two in the morning and where? Who would get us up? We left a good many notes to each other on the stair during the next few days, and by that time everyone in the hotel was discussing the astronomic event. In our correspondence, however, we were not so concerned with the event itself as with our approach to it.

And then one morning Mother, with whom I had had no conversation on the subject, asked if I would like to have a comet-seeing party on the coming Friday and invite all my friends to spend the night. The linen room would furnish cots to put up for the boys in an unoccupied room next door to our apartment and for the girls in Brother's and my room. Brother would be taken care of and housed by friends down the hall. Mother and Father would occupy their own room but wake us up in plenty of time to dress and go out with them on the Midway to see the comet. It was a scheme of breathtaking magnitude, and it left me speechless, but not for long. I rushed to tell my friends and

learned to my stupefaction that their parents had already
been approached and had consented. I had never in my life
had one friend to spend the night, and here I was moving
from nothing at all to a convention.

We assembled in our apartment after supper on the night
that finally came round. Everyone brought an extra coat for
the early-morning or late-at-night arising; we had a con-

siderable discussion over which it was. Our rooms were con-
gested; it was hard for the girls to find places for their
clothes; the boys said they would just dump theirs on the
floor. We held considerable intermural communication after
we had all finally been put to bed. We had achieved a fairly
understandable code when my parents, coming in for the
tenth time or more and speaking in strained, tight voices,
promised that if there were one more pound on the wall, or
shout out the window to interpret the pounding, we would
not be ALLOWED to see the comet.

Around one o'clock we dropped off, and at two Mother
and Father woke us, supervised our dressing, and took us

down through the quiet corridors, the dimly lighted lobby and across the spooky veranda where some of the empty chairs rocked a little and creaked in a breeze. And then there we stood, out on the Midway at a quarter to three o'clock in the morning. That was a moment for our group. After we had savored it, we looked up into the sky toward the spot the newspapers had designated. A group of people from the hotel was already assembled near ours. We could see blurred shapes, and voices called out to us. Father had brought with him a map of the sky, cut from the newspaper, and a flashlight. What his flashlight showed, apart from the map and something of the friends who gathered round to share it, was an overcast sky. Fifteen or twenty minutes later rain fell. Everyone retreated to the veranda, and our group was fairly quiet there, though Mother and Father kept hissing that we were waking everyone in the hotel who was not on the veranda with us.

At four o'clock we all gave up and went indoors. In the lobby I could see that some of the comet watchers were oddly dressed and that all of them were in drooping spirits, complaining about lack of sleep and the fizzle the comet had been.

My comet party was not in drooping spirits; we considered the occasion entirely successful. From the drawings we had been shown, a comet hadn't seemed to any of us so remarkable a sight as to warrant all the fuss about it. But we had agreed in private meetings that we would insist that the comet was the one thing in the world we most wanted to see in order to accomplish getting up at two A.M., and we had pulled it off. It was after *four* in the morning, and we were in the lobby of the hotel, fully dressed.

We did not return to bed. Singly, we would have *been* returned by the force of parental authority, but in our

This was a triumphant invasion and we enjoyed it.

union there was strength. We were up and we stayed up, overriding my parents' expostulations and orders, in itself an exhilarating experience. Those parents of my guests who had got up to see the comet left without their children because the children insisted that they were at a party and that the party wasn't over yet. They'd been invited to spend the night, and the night wasn't finished.

Father said loudly that it was finished as far as he was concerned, but Mother hushed him. One or two of the other fathers on their way to the elevator told mine that he had certainly let himself in for something, that they were sorry they couldn't help him out, but that they had to get their sleep. Father told them all to go jump in the lake, and when the last of the comet watchers not in our party had gone, he sat down on a chair in the lobby and glared at Mother, holding his hands on either side of his head. All my guests were milling around, but I edged as near Mother and Father as I judged feasible. I was interested in their lack of grip on a situation. It was the first time I had seen this, and I wanted to take as much advantage of it as I dared.

Father said to Mother, "I doubt if I'll live through the day so I might as well do anything now that you suggest. I only hope for your own sake that after I'm dead, you'll never have another idea like this jamboree of Hottentots."

Mother said she hoped she never would, but that they must take care of this one.

"Organize games," she said, "so the Hottentots won't get out of hand."

Father's eyes nearly popped out of his head.

"*Games?*" he said. "*Now?* Couldn't you tell them stories?" he added. "You're a wonderful storyteller. I've always said so, and I could sit here and listen."

I eased away from my parents and reported to my party

that we were going to play games. My guests were enthusiastic and, under my coaching, vetoed stories.

There was not room for us, dressed, in the Kimbrough rooms, of course, so we took over the lobby. We had never before had it to ourselves. As a matter of accuracy, whenever more than two or three of us were gathered together, we'd been chased out of it. This was a triumphant invasion and we enjoyed it. We slid on the polished floor, played tag around the pillars, did distance jumps from the top of the main desk, and raced against Pauline. We preferred these to the games Mother and Father suggested so we made them umpires, rousing Father up on his feet whenever he tried to fill the job sitting down.

At half-past six the dining room opened. Mother and Father lined us up outside the doors at twenty-five minutes past. The doors were scarcely half-open before they were shoving us through. The captain was surprised to see us; he hadn't known about the comet party. The waiters were surprised, too. We all sat at my family's table, and we had a very large breakfast.

The minute we'd finished, Father jumped up and began shaking hands with my guests, saying that my comet party was over and that they could go home. But they said they didn't want to, they were having such a good time, and that nobody would go to sleep now. Father said loudly that HE would if anyone would give him the chance. Mother stepped in. She told Father she didn't think he would be thanked by the other parents for returning their children at this hour. It would be wiser, she said, to hang on a little longer. Father submitted to this because, he said, he was too near the end to protest or even care. But he begged to be treated with just a fraction of the consideration being shown other parents. Would we please not come near him?

At eight he and Mother went up in the elevator. We repaired to the Ordinary. We couldn't go outside because it was still raining.

Perhaps we felt the least little bit tired. We didn't play any more games, but we discussed ways in which the group could have a round of night festivities without depending on a comet. At eight-thirty we had a second breakfast, and after that we scattered for the regular Saturday-morning activities: music lessons, dentist, et cetera. I conceded then that the party was over.

I was roused up a few nights later by my parents and taken out on the Midway again. The sky was clear and I saw the comet. It looked like the pictures of it. The guests from my comet party were there, too, but with their own parents. As far as I was concerned there was nothing about the night to remember except the humiliation of having my five-year-old brother up, dressed, and out on the Midway with us at half-past two in the morning.

4. Our Club

THE IDEA OF ORGANIZING A CLUB CAME TO ME ONE morning about a week after the comet party. We were playing in the Ordinary because the day was rainy and were talking about the good luck the rain had brought us the night we hadn't seen the comet. Had it been clear, we pointed out to one another, we'd have looked at the comet and then gone back to bed, probably in our own rooms. The party would have been over, and it was the party that had been fun, not a streak in the sky. One of the boys said he wished we could have more parties like that without having to wait for a comet.

"People do," I told him, "in Muncie, and I never heard of a comet there."

I went on to explain that in Muncie my parents had participated in group activities constantly. Allowing for the basic and incontrovertible fact that Muncie was a place a million times better than Chicago, some of its advantages might be imitated on a lesser scale. I cited the parties Mother had been to, with and without Father, just before we'd left, even including the erratic occasion of my mother in a dress suit at the Houseboat on the Styx. But I did not mention the costumes.

35

"What did you say it was?" one of the boys asked.

"The Dante Class," I told him. "They read Dante. I've seen the books. They read lots of books. That's what it was for, to read books they'd never got around to reading. But they had parties, like this comet party. So did the Conversation Club and the Art League."

The idea sprang full-panoplied.

"That's it," I added, and I was shouting. "They had clubs. That's what we need, a club, so we can stay up late and have parties. Refreshments. That's what a club is."

There was instantaneous and ungrudging enthusiasm for the idea from everybody. I made use of it to appoint myself organizer and president of whatever the club would be.

"It has to be some *kind* of a club," I explained. "I'll think up what it will be."

Somebody suggested the appointment of other officers, but I convinced them it was unnecessary. I would be able, I said, to handle everything. I would call a meeting within a few days and report the purpose of the club.

Bower became my councilor at once. I did not give her a title of office, lest it seem a precedent for the appointment of others, and the whole thing get out of hand, mine. But I knew that for the carrying out of any idea Bower was indispensable. There were notes under the carpet on the stair riser every few hours during the following days. She vetoed my suggestion of a Book Club. Boys didn't read, she said. My suggestion of an Art League, she assured me, was worse. The boys would think it sissy. A Conversation Club? She wrote, "Boys don't talk."

Those were the only clubs I knew because they were the ones to which Mother had belonged. The whole enterprise seemed to be dying at birth. And then one day Mother took Bower and me to the Field Museum. We saw there, among the exhibits, a large hunk of chewing gum in the raw. A dreadful sight—so large I could scarcely have got my two arms around it had I been allowed—lumpy, and a sickly color that was no color. We shuddered and could scarcely be persuaded to leave it for other displays.

All the way home we discussed the dark situation that had been revealed to us: people chewing gum in ignorance. If they knew the gruesome look of it, we said, before it was fixed up in packages, they would never put it in their mouths.

"We ought to tell them," I said and stopped. On Fifty-ninth Street and Lake Park Avenue I received the call to duty. Like Joan of Arc I knew what I must do and how I could do it.

"That's what the club will be," I announced when speech was restored to me after this revelation. "We'll keep people from chewing gum. It will be the Anti-Gum Society."

Bower agreed almost at once. The fact that she could find no reason why this scheme could not be carried out sealed my conviction that its conception was supernatural.

"It was Fate," I pronounced.

Reaching the hotel, we found the group assembled, as usual, on the Midway. We were unable to distract the members from a brisk round of sample trading that was occupying their attention until Bower went upstairs and brought down a box of Tootsie Rolls. By a judicious distribution of these we secured a hearing and I explained the mission that had been revealed to me.

Their response to it was very like what Joan of Arc got when she explained at court what the voices had told her to do. The boys of my group said that an anti-gum society was the silliest thing they'd ever heard of. Gum was fine. Phil Bergstresser insisted that probably everything you ate looked awful at some time or other; Stuffy Reber shouted that this was a false statement, and then he was drowned out by everybody yelling things like who cared if people wanted to chew gum no matter how it looked? And how were you going to stop them, even if you wanted to? And a club was for having fun. Where would the fun be?

The difference between Joan of Arc and me was that Joan had no Bower. Bower said to me that if I could get everybody quiet, she would tell them a few things. I could shout as loud as the boys and longer than any of them; that was acknowledged in the group. I got them quiet. Bower told them then that the best way to stop people from doing things was to fine them if they did, like spitting on the Illinois Central trains or throwing trash around in the park. We could start with everybody in the hotel. We'd ask them to pay a fine every time they chewed gum; we could maybe march up and down with signs telling about the way gum looked, and after that we would take up a collection.

The boys began to be interested. One of them asked what we'd do with the money if we did collect fines. Bower was ready for that. We could give it to Dr. Black, she suggested, for his children's heart hospital. Dr. Black was the hotel doctor and one of our favorite people. This seemed a noble purpose to the majority, but Stuffy modified it. We could give half to the doctor, he proposed, and keep the other half for the club as payment for the work we'd done. Out of that we could buy refreshments for the club meetings. That was the way it was finally decided, over Bower's protests and offer to furnish Tootsie Rolls at her father's expense.

We began the signs the next day. The laundry and kitchen provided us with pieces of cardboard. Bower and I each had a box of water colors. The work was done on the Midway at

Father said a man faced with vaccination was a sucker for anything.

the spot where the trading post had been. There was a slight delay in the beginning because we couldn't decide what to say on the signs. Eventually we settled on,

"Clean Up Chicago. Don't Chew Gum."

"Gum Is Disgusting."

"Help the Babies. Don't Chew."

"Fine for Chewing. Pay the Club."

And they were all signed, "The Anti-Gum Society."

When the signs were finished, and we were bickering about the time to hold the parade, Fate, as I said to Bower, came in again.

An employee of the hotel developed smallpox and was rushed off to "The Pest House." Someone told us that name, and we were all fascinated by it, evoking among ourselves an institution something like the Black Hole of Calcutta, an insane asylum, and the Debtor's Prison.

Dr. Black decreed that everyone in the hotel must be vaccinated. He drafted two nurses from a nearby hospital, had announcements posted in the lobby, elevators, kitchen; no department escaped. He set the hour for the operation— six P.M.—and the place—the hotel lobby—since his office would be far too small. This was the hour, I said, for the parade. And that is when we held it.

As the patients lined up in a serpentine that wound all around the room—guests and employees, young and old— our club members swept in from the Ordinary, blowing a rousing tune on combs and beating with spoons on tin trays. The posters were pinned on us, front and rear; we attracted a gratifying quota of attention and an even more gratifying percentage of subscriptions when we took up a collection immediately following the procession. Father said afterward a man faced with a vaccination was a sucker for anything; he wouldn't even know what he was being

asked, he'd just comply. He added that an insurance sales-
man could have cleaned up.

Father may have been right because we never had so
successful a collection again, but we did have a wonderful
feast on that one. And our vaccinations didn't take.

In a short time we were discouraged to find that the field
in which our parents had placed us was not profitable for
anti-gum solicitation. None of the adult guests in the hotel
chewed gum; the only young ones who did were members
of our society. Bower, Pauline, and I had never been allowed
to chew it, and the boys refused to continue paying fines to
buy refreshments for us.

It was less than two weeks later that I left a note in our
special place for Bower. The note was written in red crayon.

"The Club Is Going To Perish," it read. "Meet me at
six by the elevator."

We conferred there at six, sitting on the steps around the
corner from the elevator. I was gloomy. We had not, I felt,
broken the chewing gum industry. There was no money in
the treasury; the only gum-chewing sources of revenue had
quit. Bower agreed with my summing up. Things looked
bad, she told me, and asked if I had any ideas.

That was what I'd been leading up to. There was only
one hope, I declared, and that was to enlarge the purpose
of the organization. Gum was too limited; we had proven
that. Therefore we must find something in addition that
had a wider appeal and something everyone would know
about—like Literature, for instance.

Bower didn't think much of the enlargement by way of
Literature, but just that once I overrode her, and at an
urgency meeting of the club I talked the members into it.
They said they didn't see how we were going to get money
out of Literature. I promised I would think up something.

The point I kept driving through to them was that we didn't want the club to die, and it was going to die unless we enlarged it to a subject that would include everybody. I recited again and again the names of the clubs in Muncie to which my Mother had belonged and pointed out that each of them had something to do with Literature, and each one kept alive without any trouble at all. Literature was what did it. The members conceded the point. The club was saved, and its name was changed.

What followed remained for a long time a mystery to me. I referred to it as Fate. Money came in for the club in larger sums than we had ever got for the gum campaign except on the day of the parade, and this new money came in unsolicited.

Bower and I would be walking through the lobby and a guest—sometimes a whole group of people sitting there—would summon us. The proposal was always the same. The spokesman would say something like, "I've been hearing about a club you children have formed. I'm not sure that I've got it straight, though. If you will tell me what you do at your club and what the name of it is, I'll make a contribution to it."

Bower or I would answer gladly, and our answer was always the same, of course.

"We bring books to read. Everybody brings the book he is reading and goes on reading it, and there are refreshments to eat while you read.

"The name of the club is The Anti-Gum and Literary Society."

5. The Other Side of the Tracks

AFTER A FEW MONTHS AT THE DEL PRADO MY PARENTS began to question their choice of a hotel as a good place in which to bring up children. They cited, in my overhearing, some of the reasons for this. One was our waiter's solicitude over my eating. He always brought me a serving of every meat listed on the menu, and though we all knew that after I had given my imperial nod of selection, the other meats would be slipped into the specially lined coat pocket of his suit and taken home to his family, Mother and Father called the practice an unsuitable way in which to present a meal to a child. Certainly for me it was a far and joyful cry from the dreary and daily admonition in Muncie to "Eat what's put before you, Emily, and every scrap of it, or no dessert." Here almost everything was set before me for my selection, and I ate as much as I wanted of all the desserts.

"As if that were not enough," Mother told my father, "both the children have the bellboys fetching and carrying for them until you might think we had produced a pair of Indian potentates. I forbid them to ask anything of a bell-boy, but all the other children do it. And Brother's getting too much attention from all the old ladies. It's because of his looks so I can't blame the child for that. Of course Emily's in no danger of spoiling on that score. But they're both of them so changed I dread to think what your mother and father would say if we took them back to Muncie now. This is the worst possible environment for them."

That was the general theme of conversation that I listened to in the evening and longed to join in order to say that if environment meant what I thought it did, I considered Brother's and mine altogether lovely. Listening to conversations between my parents was one of its charms. In Muncie I had been put to bed too far from the living room for any participation, but at the Del Prado Brother's and my bedroom adjoined the sitting room. Only a little care was necessary in order not to make a noise when I eased out of bed. After that it was simply a matter of sitting quietly on the floor with my ear against the door to put myself *au courant* with the fascinating and hitherto unrevealed things that adults discussed when children were told to run away because the grown-ups were talking.

I could have mentioned many other aspects of this environment that made me consider it idyllic, but they all seemed to me to be the very things about which my parents were complaining. I repeated their complaints to Bower and added that I was afraid Mother and Father were going to do something about them. In my vocabulary, for my parents to do something about a situation was to do something bad or at least to Brother's and my disadvantage. Bower made light of my misgivings. Parents, she assured me, were always in a condition of not liking something. After they got tired of not liking the way we ate the food, they would probably not like the food. Her parents, she said, did that every once in a while, complained to the manager about the meals, and then in no time were back at her again for rolling her bread into pills and eating it that way. As for our ordering everything on the menu, if we didn't do that, how were the waiters going to get extra food to take home? Parents understood practically nothing at all.

I was so lulled by this picture of martyred superiority that for a week or two after this conversation I did not keep a sharp ear to the door, preferring to improvise, in my bed, conversations with my parents in which, with patience, I broadened their range of understanding and brought them to a humble and grateful appreciation of their children.

Therefore when Mother and Father took Brother and me for a walk in Jackson Park one Sunday afternoon and told us, there, that we were going to move from the hotel to an apartment of our own, I was shocked. In the next ten seconds I was violently and deafeningly antagonistic to the idea. Anticipation of this may have been the reason Mother and Father had chosen the large, open site of Jackson Park for imparting the news.

When I was able to shape my roars into words, I assured them that there wasn't another family in the world capable of doing such a thing to their children. Mother pointed out that, on the contrary, many parents did just that, naming specifically the Nitzes. She could not have made a poorer selection, as I explained to her at the top of my lungs. Dr. and Mrs. Nitze had recently moved into the Del Prado. Dr. Nitze was to be a professor at the University of Chicago. They had lived in Germany. They had two children, Elizabeth and Paul. Elizabeth was younger than I, and Paul was practically a baby and could only speak German. How could Brother and I possibly be like those children? I scarcely even talked to Elizabeth because she was younger, and nobody could talk to Paul. Denied this privilege of association, they probably were unhappy at the Del Prado and so their parents were taking them away. Brother and I were perfectly happy.

I turned to Brother for support. I very rarely turned to him for anything, choosing rather to avoid him as much as possible, but this was a crisis, and he had said nothing at all. When I appealed to him, he pronounced slowly and ruminatively that as long as we stayed near enough the Illinois Central tracks so that he could see the trains go by, he wouldn't care if we moved. He didn't like eating in the Ordinary anyway. Deliberating further, he added that maybe if we moved he wouldn't have to be cleaned up so much nor be polite to so many people. How soon could we go?

This repudiation removed again, for a moment, my ability to speak. Regaining it, I assured him that I might have known he would be a stinkweed and that I hoped with all my heart I would never have to speak to him again as long as I lived. I then implored my parents to allow me to stay on at the Del Prado. The Kellys, I felt confident, would be delighted to adopt me, and I would like nothing better than to change my name and be Bower's sister, seeing my parents perhaps, but not Brother, at Christmas. I derived a crumb of comfort from the impression that Mother was distressed by this proposal, but Father said briskly that there was to be no further discussion of the subject. It had been decided. They had thought, during this walk, to show us the apartment selected. It was near by, but perhaps we would prefer to be surprised. We'd be moving into it on Wednesday. The furniture was coming out of storage. All our old familiar things from Muncie would be installed and waiting for us when we arrived.

I was not surprised when Brother broke in, demanding that we go at once to see the apartment. My only comment

The trains seemed to go through our kitchen.

on this toadying was to observe that I knew a person, not far away from me, that made anyone completely sick just to look at.

Mother, Father, and Brother struck off briskly across the park, I dragging miserably behind them. We came to a street only a block long. Father said, "Well, here we are. This is it."

Mother explained that she and Father had come upon it on one of their walks and had thought immediately how nice it would be to live there because it was quiet, since no traffic ran through it, and particularly because it was so filled with children. There would be lots of playmates for both of us. "I call it 'Good Children's Street,' " she added. That was a poem by Eugene Field. Brother and I both knew it. But I saw nothing good about the street nor the apartment they pointed out that was to be ours. My eyes were too blurred from weeping for clear vision, but anyone could have seen that this was simply a red brick building with a porch in front of each apartment. We couldn't get in to see ours because Father didn't have a key and the janitor was out. I turned my back on it and stared moodily at a group of children playing across the street.

All the way home Brother jabbered idiotically about how he was going to set up his Meccano and his electric trains again because he was told that in this apartment he would have a room of his own.

The instant we were in the hotel I telephoned Bower to meet me at once on the stairs beside the elevator. I couldn't take time to leave a note in our special place.

I told her the terrible news and she was stricken. She received more stoically the information that my family would not allow her parents to adopt me. But she protested that we would always be best friends. I knew better, and so

did she. Once a child left the hotel, he never was part of
the group again. We'd seen it happen, over and over. A girl
or boy would come back to play. They always seemed to
have become strangers to us and after one or two visits
would drop out altogether.

Brother's and mine were the only expectations completely
realized by the new apartment. He had wanted it close to
the Illinois Central tracks, and it was—so close that the
trains seemed to go through our kitchen. Mother admitted,
even to me, that she had allowed the renting agent to whisk
her around the kitchen on a brief whirl, and lead her only
a step or two out on the back porch, where he'd directed her
attention to the pleasant yard below our second-floor location. He had, by this ruse, diverted her attention from the
railroad tracks, separated only by a wall from the end of
our yard. She confessed, too, to a reluctant admiration for
his skillful timing of her inspection of that section of the
apartment at one of the infrequent periods of the day when
trains were not passing. Father, brought over to give his
opinion before the lease was signed, had not gone near the
kitchen and had only said that if Mother liked the flat, he
thought it was fine. She remonstrated with him about this
later but got no satisfaction.

I reiterated, and was frequently sent to my room for it,
the fulfillment of my expectations. I had said it would be
lonely to live in an apartment, I pointed out, and it was—
especially in this one. Mother had been as misled by the
children she saw in front of the apartment as by not having
seen the Illinois Central tracks. "Good Children's Street"
she had called it. The children were there, but they were
anything but good. Most of them were terrors. In almost no
time Brother and I were forbidden to play with all but a
very few. Furthermore, she had not stopped to wonder why

the children were clustered on the steps of the buildings, as we had seen them the day we visited the street. Brother and I had joined them before she perceived that it was because we had nowhere else to play.

In Muncie there had been yards, front, side, and back— swings in the side yard, playhouses in the back. At the Del Prado there had been the whole Midway on which to have our games. But these apartments had only a back yard, and more times than not it was a stone court and not a yard at

all. Ours did have grass, brown, dry, and gritty underfoot because of the constant rain of cinders from the train.

"Why didn't I think of these things?" Mother said one night when we were all at supper, and she was very close to tears. "I seem to have a mind that only works in an environment I'm used to. When I come to a strange one, I don't seem even to know how to choose a place to live in. There are such different things to think about here."

And so she took Brother and me on an excursion every day to get away from the apartment and the noisy street. It was late summer, hot and dry; even the park was dusty. We were too far from the Del Prado to walk there every day. Mother took me twice. I played with our friends while Mother visited with Mrs. Kelly, but my friends were concentrated on a new special game that I didn't know. They had stopped trading samples and the club was disbanded. I knew it was going to be like this. When Mother suggested another visit there, I told her I didn't like the hotel any more.

She took Brother and me to the Field Museum in Jackson Park, again and again. Sometimes we went farther to see the lake, but the lake was a long walk from where we lived, and a breakwater along that part of it made swimming impossible. The beach, still farther away, was crowded and frequented by gangs of rough boys that made Mother uneasy. We didn't belong to any clubs. They had private beaches. So we didn't go swimming.

Mother began to take us into Chicago to the Art Institute in the afternoons. She made up games to play there, with rewards. When we walked in Jackson Park she would point out the way clouds looked on that particular day, or the lake, or almost anything we saw, and would tell us the name of a painter who particularly liked to paint them that way. Then, when we got into the Art Institute, she would offer a prize to the one who would be the first to find pictures painted by those artists. Brother and I liked this diversion a good deal, though Brother was equally partial to sliding on the stone floors. Father would come from his office, after work, meet us there, and we'd all go home together on the Illinois Central train. If he got away early enough to take us to Huylers' for a soda before Mother said it would spoil our supper, the day was a total success.

The rewards themselves for the pictures identified were worth while; Brother and I both conceded that. They included a trip to Marshall Field and Company and a selection of a toy, within a limited price range, from the toy department on the fourth floor. The Marshall Field excursion required an entire afternoon in itself; it could never be combined with the Art Institute. And so, between the two objectives, we visited the city three or four times a week. This, too, troubled Mother. Going home on the train one late afternoon, she said to Father, "This way of living isn't much better for the children than the Del Prado. It's elaborate and artificial. What's the matter with us, Hal? Other people move to a city and seem to slip into it. Are we misfits? Or do you suppose it's as hard for them, too?"

Father said that maybe we were trying to swallow too much of the city in one gulp and that it was too strong a dose for us. Maybe it ought to be diluted a little for the children, me especially. How about having one or two Muncie friends come to visit me for a week? I'd fall right back into the Muncie pattern, simple amusements, games among ourselves, and a few excursions to show them the city. Then I'd see it from a new point of view. This was the best idea Father had ever had, and I told him so, vociferously. Mother seemed stumped by it. While I was developing the suggestions that came rapidly to my mind, she sat staring at him in silence. But in the middle of an inspired amplification that I was proposing to Father she interrupted.

"Hush, Emily," she said, "at least for a minute. Let me talk to your father."

I allowed her this interlude because it permitted me to enlarge my ideas to really ample proportions. I was so preoccupied by this that I paid little attention to what she was saying, only vaguely aware that she was somewhat disturbed by Father's making the suggestion in front of me without their having talked it over first between them. I was aware that this was the first time such a thing had happened and considered there was added charm in the idea because of its freshness. It had not been worried to shreds between them before I had been let in on it.

Father admitted that he had surprised himself by making the suggestion but felt that since he was responsible for our being in Chicago, he must do something, quickly, to make it more palatable. Mother insinuated a few difficulties. Perhaps the parents wouldn't allow the children to come. Our sleeping accommodations were limited, and what would she do about Brother while she devoted herself to me and my guests? He would not lend himself willingly to the things that would be fun to us. The maid, recently engaged, was none too dependable. And there you were again, back at another of the difficulties in a city. You didn't have neighbors, friends, to whom you could turn over your child as a matter of course.

I emerged from my reverie of the giddy round that I was planning and heard with anguish the continuing list of difficulties. But as I was gathering my forces together to fight this obstacle, Mother, having listed the difficulties, announced that she would solve them. This was the first time, as far as I knew, that anything had come my way without my fighting for it. The realization that during an interval when I was not talking something that I most wanted was granted astonished me. I thought about it all the rest of the way home, while Mother and Father went on to discuss pleasures for Brother to compensate for the treat in store for me, Brother listening, approving, and making occasional suggestions. It broke over me then that this was the way it always was with Brother. He never clamored and shouted. He simply waited, acting as if he didn't care at all. In the end he always got as much as I, frequently, it seemed to me, more than I.

Walking home from the station, I considered asking him

about this, but I didn't want to give him the satisfaction of telling me something. And, furthermore, I came to the conclusion that his was a method I would find unsympathetic and would not care to risk.

The two little girls were invited, Louise Carey and Marian Miltenberger, and their parents written to. Beginning with the morning the letters were mailed, I waited for the postman at the corner an hour before the time of each of the two daily deliveries.

But before the answers came, we suddenly made friends with the family across the hall from us. We knew that the family included a mother, father, and three sons, and that their name was Hart. They had been away when we moved in, and on their return Mother and Father had exchanged a good morning, or evening, when they met. But the boys and I had not even said hello until the middle one, practicing in the back yard one afternoon with a new air rifle, used me as a target. Specifically, he aimed at that part of me presented to him at a distance of about fifteen feet when I, headed in the opposite direction, stooped over on the first-floor landing of the back stairs to retrieve a roller skate I had dropped. He achieved a bull's eye, and though the BB shot that I received did no actual damage, the contact, and my reception of it, broke immediately the ice between the two families.

We learned that Percival was a little older than I, Richard, the marksman, was younger, and William was Brother's age. Owing to the circumstance of our introduction, the relationship between Richard and me remained on a basis of formality and strain. But Percival and I became friends, that is, he was nice to me and I looked up to him with awe because he had read so many books. There were no qualifying elements in the combination between Brother and

"Avaunt, if you don't want to get fired."

William. They said hello to each other when the family came over to apologize for Richard's pot shot of the afternoon; they retired immediately to Brother's room to see his electric train and summoned by Mr. and Mrs. Hart at the end of their call, William stayed instead with us, for supper.

Percival had some Howard Pyle books that I hadn't read, and the next day he loaned them to me. He also had books by Dickens that were his very own and that he was reading. This seemed to me on a plane with Bower's silver toilet set. I had only one volume of Dickens, the child's version, and cared very little for it. He still liked the Howard Pyle, however, so we read together some of the stories, taking turns reading aloud.

We were reading one afternoon, a day or so later, when our maid heard me ask him what a privy closet was. There was a line in the Howard Pyle *King Arthur* to the effect that Queen Guinevere had repaired to her privy closet in sorrow. Percival, or Perk as he was called, told me it was a private council chamber in the castle. But when he went home, our maid said that I had been talking nasty to him and she was going to tell my mother on me. She wouldn't explain what it was but kept saying, "You know very well what you said."

I was filled with shame and embarrassment, and next day I hid when he came over to ask for me. I hid in the linen closet. This was quite a large room but without a window. Because the door was always kept closed, the place seemed cooler than the rest of the apartment. I read a good deal in there, lying on a shelf on top of the bath towels and squeezed under the shelf above. I pulled down beside me the electric light bulb that hung on a flexible cord from the ceiling. Concealed, the light did not shine through under the door so I could remain undetected, somewhat at peace.

Perk was the first one to discover my reading nook. He came over to our apartment the following day, walked down the hall looking for me, and opened the door of the linen closet. He said he thought it was a fine place so I invited him in. He was able to fit under a shelf after we took the sheets from the one he wanted to lie on, but his legs dangled off the end, and he wasn't very comfortable. The maid came along while we were trying to set up a pile of sheets tall enough to put under his feet. She heard us talking and opened the door. The next minute she was screaming at us that she was going to tell our mothers and we would certainly catch it.

I was scared of her. She was red in the face, rolling her eyes, and yelling. But Perk walked up to her and said, very loud, "Hold your tongue, or I'll report you."

And she did stop yelling.

Then he took my hand, "like Sir Tristram," I said to myself later. He led me past the maid and down the hall, but at the door to the living room he called back over his shoulder to her, "Avaunt, if you don't want to get fired."

I told Mother and Father all about it that night at supper. They agreed that Perk had been like Sir Tristram. The next day he rose in my estimation from Sir Tristram to an inhabitant of Mount Olympus because the maid *was* fired. While he was occupying that site, the letters finally arrived from the parents of my friends, and I left him there. Marian and Louise were coming. I was raucous with excitement, rushing up and down the hall of the apartment proclaiming the news.

When Perk came over with two books on that morning, I told him he might as well take them back. We were getting a new maid, company was coming to visit me. Under the circumstances, I explained, he and literature would have to wait.

6. Visitors From Home

MOTHER AND I MET MY GUESTS AT THE ENGLEWOOD Station. We arrived there, because of my insistence that we would be late, one half hour before the train was due. While we waited, I rehearsed again all of the things the girls and I were going to do and some of the things we were going to say to one another. I had walked away from Mother while I was thinking, and she called to me, "Here they come."

The train was coasting in. I raced down the platform toward it, but when it stopped, Mother was at the steps of their coach. I saw them step down from it and kiss her. I ran to them. They didn't kiss me, and I didn't know how to accomplish kissing them, so I stood beside Mother. Marian said, "Hello, Emily."

I said, "Hello, Marian. Hello, Louise."

After that Mother asked them to show her which were their suitcases so that she could tell the redcap. Later, walking along the platform behind the porter, I said, "You're both wearing your hair the same way you used to."

Marian answered, "So are you."

Marian's hair was dark and she wore it in braids. Louise's was blond, and her braids were long and thick. I told them this was Englewood Station, and Marian said they knew that. I asked how everything was in Muncie, and Marian said fine. I asked how their mother and father were, and Marian said fine. By this time we had been together about fifteen minutes, and I couldn't think of anything else to ask them.

In the cab I told the girls how wonderful it was to live in a big city and some of the things they were going to see. Marian said that would be fine. She added that her mother had said living in a city would drive her crazy. She was certainly glad it wasn't their family that had moved. I told her we just loved it. Mother did all the talking the rest of the way home.

The three of us shared my room. I showed the girls their space in the closet and bureau, and I took them all over the apartment. They were interested in the button that clicked the lock to open the door downstairs and the speaking tube beside it, but Marian said it was funny to be upstairs and yet on one floor. I asked if they'd like to walk up and down the street, but they said they'd rather unpack.

While they were unpacking, I wandered into the living room and picked up one of the two books that Perk had left. They were *The Jungle Book* and *The Second Jungle Book*, I saw, by Rudyard Kipling. I began to read the first story in the first book.

Halfway through it I said to myself, "This is the most wonderful book in the world."

Mother came in and asked what on earth I was doing. I showed her the book. She took it out of my hand and said sharply that I must go to my guests. I went to my room and asked what they would like to do; they'd finished unpacking. They said they'd like to write letters so I fixed a place for them at each end of my desk. I went back to the living room. Mother wasn't there and neither were *The Jungle Books*. I couldn't find Mother or the books. I went back to my room and waited for Marian and Louise to finish their letters. We walked to the corner and mailed them.

Before supper that night William came in with Brother. Mrs. Hart had taken care of both boys for the entire day.

"I feel as if I were in Muncie again, with a neighbor," Mother said over and over to her when Mrs. Hart delivered Brother, and Mother insisted that William come in with Brother. "That will give you a little chance to get your breath," she told Mrs. Hart.

Mother announced to the boys that she had a story to read to them, and produced *The Second Jungle Book*. She read "The White Seal." I listened. When she had finished the boys said one after the other, "Read it again."

"Read it again."

She read it all over again and then said there was time before supper for one more story.

"How about 'Little Toomai of the Elephants'?"

The boys said, "Read 'The White Seal' again."

She did.

After supper I asked for the books.

"Not until your guests have gone," she told me. I asked when that would be. I went back to Marian and Louise in my room. That was where they seemed to like to stay. I showed them my post-card album.

The next day we went to Jackson Park and saw the Japanese buildings, there since the World's Fair. We saw the lake the same day, and on the next, the Field Museum. The following days we went in town to the Art Institute, and we visited Marshall Field's twice. I had learned to play jacks. I showed the game to the girls, but they didn't care much for it. No one in Muncie, they said, played it. They

We even had lunch at Marshall Field's.

reminded me of a game we'd played there. "How-many-miles-to-Banbury-Cross. Three-score-and-ten-can-I-get-there-by-candle-light. Yes-and-back-again. Look-out-the-witches-don't-catch-you." But that game required a good deal of room, with enough people to make two good teams. The ones I had learned they didn't know, and the ones they knew we couldn't play because you couldn't cut them down to fit Chicago. They liked looking at my collection of samples and my post-card album and my set of cardboard furniture and paper dolls. So I gave them all those things to look at and play with and I went to the linen closet and read. But I couldn't find *The Jungle Books*.

The day before they left was to be the culmination of the whole visit. They were to buy presents and something for themselves at Marshall Field's. We spent almost the whole day in the store. We even ate in the tearoom there. We had chicken patty, green peas, and vanilla ice cream with chocolate sauce. Before we ate we made a general tour because Mother said that probably afterward we would like to stay in the toy department.

During the general tour the girls bought handkerchiefs on the first floor for their parents. That took care of the morning. After we had eaten, we settled down to selecting the toy each was going to have for her very own. We looked at dolls, doll clothes, doll furniture, all kinds of games, paints, painting books, colored chalk. Half an hour before closing time they had not yet chosen what they wanted. Mother said she was afraid we would be put out of the store. She didn't want to hurry them, but did they think they could make up their minds?

Marian said she had known what she wanted even before she left Muncie. She'd wanted to see everything else in case she should change her mind. But she hadn't changed it. What she wanted most of all was a pair of manicure scissors of her very own. Was there a place in Marshall Field's where you could get them? We went downstairs to the notion counter on the first floor. Marian selected a pair of scissors there, and Louise confided that she would rather have a little sewing box than a toy. She saw one at the notion counter just like one she'd seen at McNaughton's in Muncie. So she bought that.

They went home the next morning. Perk came over that afternoon and Mother gave me back *The Jungle Books*. We read "Little Toomai of the Elephants." It was wonderful.

The following week Mother told me that we were going to move to another apartment. She said someone else was going to take this one off our hands, and she hoped they would enjoy it. Her conscience was clear because, she said, she had pointed across the back yard to the Illinois Central tracks when she had showed them the kitchen.

We were going to an apartment in the building, she explained, where Aunt Nelle and Uncle Channing Ward lived. Uncle Channing came from Richmond, Virginia, but he had married Aunt Nelle, Mother's and Father's oldest friend in Muncie. They had come to Chicago to live, found an apartment, and made a much better job of it than she had, Mother said, though they hadn't been here so long as we. They had further discovered that another one in the same building was going to be vacant and had got it for us. Aunt Nelle and Mother would go to concerts together and to lectures at the University of Chicago. Mother looked gayer than I'd seen her for a long time. Aunt Nelle was a wonderful musician, Mother added, and had said she would give me piano lessons. I would go to Miss Faulkner's School for Girls that was only three blocks away, and Brother would start at the Kenwood Public School only one block from the apartment. It would all be lovely, and we would never hear a train again unless we were on it.

The plan did not appeal to me, but I decided I didn't really care much. I'd only made friends with Perk Hart. In bed that night I thought a long time about people moving to a city. Once they started, they never seemed to stop. And everything about them got farther and farther away from how it had been when they started.

7. Brother's Social Life

T HE ONLY SETBACK TO BROTHER'S ACCLIMATIZATION TO
Chicago was the attack of whooping cough on his arrival. The moment he was released from the confinement
it imposed, he explored his environment and settled into
it promptly. He also began, almost immediately, a business
career by telling a very stout gentleman at the Del Prado
whether or not his shoes were properly shined each morning, and receiving a penny in payment for the service.
Mother put a stop to these transactions as soon as she
learned about them, but in the meantime he had gathered
a neat sum.

Apart from money, his main interest was engines, or
anything mechanical. Any base that provided him with
opportunity to pursue both of these was, therefore, completely satisfactory to him. When income from the fat man
ceased, Brother turned his attention to mechanics. After
familiarizing himself thoroughly with the hotel laundry
and the boiler room, he asked to be taken daily to see the
trains on the Illinois Central tracks near by.

At supper, Mother reporting to Father the events of the
day, frequently questioned the benefit from her outings
with him.

"We sit on a bench at the station," she would explain, "in a constant and over-all vibration as those trains thunder past us. My eyes smart from the smoke, we are peppered with cinders, and what we breathe is certainly not fresh air, it isn't even air, it's fumes."

She pointed out another time that in Muncie to see one fast train a day had satisfied Brother, since it was the only one there was. A further example, she insisted, of how much simpler daily living was in a small town.

While we were still at the Del Prado, a group of professors from the University of Chicago set up a tent near by, at Sixtieth Street and Stoney Island Avenue. The purpose of the tent was to shelter an airplane which the professors proposed to construct according to a design on which they had been working. I heard Mother tell Father that she wished the professors were aware of her enthusiastic support; there was very little she would not do to encourage them to continue their work, for the reason that Brother was pleased to watch the construction of the machine in substitution for a daily visit to the tracks. Mother also said that perhaps it was quibbling on her part to mind being chased by the bulldog that the professors maintained to guard the tent. The almost daily sprint, clutching Brother by the hand, the dog rumbling at their heels, was probably good exercise, she admitted, though undignified.

In the late summer the professors removed the tent and dismantled the machine. Winter was coming on, and they had not been able to get the airplane off the ground. Mother was indifferent to their lack of success, but sincerely mourned the discontinuance of their efforts, since this threatened to drive her back to the tracks again.

Before this dismantling was completed, however, we had moved from the Del Prado to the apartment on what

Mother had called with Olympian inaccuracy, "Good Children's Street." Brother was indifferent to the children, good or bad, because he did not feel the need of companionship. He had discovered, on the day we moved into the apartment, that merely by standing on his own back porch he could watch the Illinois Central trains go by. He became a determined homebody.

But one day, coaxed and disciplined into a walk to Jackson Park, he found, on the steps of the Field Museum, two Luna moths. Escorted by Mother, and at her suggestion, he called on the head of the Museum in his office, and presented to the institution his two specimens. In spite of Mother's protests, the curator insisted on paying him five dollars apiece for the treasures. Brother instantly turned from the tracks to a concentration on his alternate interest, which was money.

He became a regular visitor to the Museum, and though he developed an academic interest in its contents, he was always careful to make a thorough survey of the approach to the building in the hope of picking up again something of monetary value. Though he did not say so, it was obvious that this was the incentive that moved him to be taken without protest on visits to the Art Institute. We could never enter the building until he had made a thorough examination of its exterior steps, that covered a very generous area. Father said, when Mother expressed her anxiety about Brother's approach to beauty, that he considered it thoroughly American, and healthy.

Mother's next anxiety about Brother was his limited circle of friends. When she told me this I felt that she was overstating the situation. You couldn't make a circle out of William Hart, I said, and William was Brother's only friend.

"You like people," Mother explained during this same conversation, "and talking. Brother likes mechanical things, and looking. I wish your interests were more evenly divided."

We didn't mention Brother's other interest.

I answered instead that I thought Brother was lucky not to have friends, that was why he didn't care how often we moved nor where we lived, as long as he could look at things. On the other hand I did care, but what was the use of making friends when I was constantly being jerked away from them?

Mother interrupted me quickly.

"You can scarcely call moving from Muncie to the Del Prado Hotel, and from the Del Prado to this apartment, 'constantly.' But when you come from a town to a city, you have to feel around and experiment a little to find just where you fit."

This conversation took place in the apartment on "Good Children's Street," and it was at this point in it that she told me we were going to move again, to Blackstone Avenue.

This apartment was very much better than the one on the tracks. It was, actually, a charming place, though nothing in the world would have induced me to admit it. The street itself in that block was heavily shaded by beautiful old trees. Our building was three stories high, and stood between two houses, each of them with a garden, and was of dark red brick with white pillars that supported porches for the apartments above the first floor. There were six apartments in all, two to a floor, and the porches for the second- and third-floor dwellers were bordered by a white railing across the front, with a solid partition between each pair. They were large enough to be furnished with a hammock or settee and a number of chairs, small tables, et cetera. All of them had flower boxes across the front, on top of the railings.

The apartments themselves were of comfortable size, the living room as large as ours had been in Muncie, and with a fireplace too, like the one in Muncie. The bedrooms were between the living and dining rooms down a hall, and the maid's room was off the kitchen.

The back porch was even larger than the front veranda, and the back yard, of considerable size, too, was edged with flower beds.

Between our building and the next house to the north of us, there was a stretch of lawn with an iron fence to mark the boundary. A driveway beside it belonged to our apartment house and led to a large barn for the use of those tenants who owned automobiles.

Although Brother had accepted imperturbably the news of another change, on the day of the moving he turned morose. On the instant of arrival he wanted to set up in his new room the tracks for his electric train, but Mother told him he would have to allow the movers to bring in the furniture first. He then asked for his Meccano set so that he could build a new bridge, and Mother said that would be all right if he would do it quietly on the front porch. But Father couldn't remember where the set had been packed and said he had other things to think about. After that Brother got in everybody's way and complained that he had nothing to do.

Mother must have felt heavily pushed, or she could not have resorted to an acknowledgment of what she considered the less commendable of Brother's two interests. She was also vexed by the number of houseflies that had entered the apartment, because of the necessity for propping open the screen of the back porch in order to allow the moving men free passage. She proposed to Brother that he catch flies. She would pay him a penny for a dozen killed. He could put them in a container and they would count the total when he had got all he could.

Brother accepted this offer and went off to the kitchen to ask our maid, Hilda, for a container. That was the last we saw of him for the entire afternoon. But when the movers had gone, and Mother and Father were having some tea in the living room, prescribed by Hilda to keep them from dying on their feet, and I was sitting near them on a rolled up rug, drinking a glass of milk, Brother appeared in the doorway. He held, clasped across his front, three quart Mason fruit jars, and they were packed to the brim with flies, presumably dead. Asked where on earth he had got them, he boasted that he had found a grocery store two blocks away. The man there had told him he could kill all the flies he wanted, and had even allowed him to scrape from the tanglesheets the ones already dead there. He had not counted the haul, he said, because Mother had told him they would do it together.

An approximated sum was paid him by Father over Mother's cries of disapproval. She declared that Brother knew she had meant for him to kill only the flies that had got into the apartment! That furthermore, he knew he was not allowed to go away from home by himself. He had gone away from home and had crossed two streets. Father countered that Mother had not specifically stated where the flies were to be killed, that Brother was going to live from now on in a city and go to a public school, and both of these changes involved more than crossing two streets. She had better begin to get used to that. Brother was, however, ordered by Father never to go away from the apartment building again without asking Mother; to discontinue, from now on, the fly-killing business, and to get rid of, immediately, the product of this initial effort.

Hilda would not accept them in the kitchen. From the living room we could hear her making this clear to him. He disappeared again. Mother and Father were too tired to look for him. They said to each other they trusted him not to leave the apartment premises again, just after he had been told specifically his boundary.

He had not left the building, but he did not return to us for an hour. We heard him then in the back of the apartment, asking in loud tones, the whereabouts of Mother. Mother called out that she and Father were exactly where he had left them, and added her doubts that they would regain sufficient strength to move from that spot for several days. I had moved to the porch but I could hear Brother clearly. It was always possible to hear Brother clearly within a considerable radius. His voice was very deep and very loud. In Muncie people had said that his voice was exactly like his Grandfather Kimbrough's. When anyone said this, Mother generally answered that though she felt this to be true, she considered the depth and volume of voice more appropriate to Grandfather Kimbrough's size and years than to Brother's.

Brother tramped into the living room, and announced in this voice that he was now the owner of a circle of friends. Their names were Lily and Rudy. Mother was delighted, and said so at once. She asked if they lived in the building and added that she would speak to their mother and father. Brother prefaced his answer by calling attention to the fact that he had been the first to produce new friends here, though he was always being accused of not having any. These friends did live in our building; in the basement. He didn't know their mother's name, but their father's name was Gus. He was our janitor. Brother had gone down-stairs, he went on to explain, sent by Hilda to dispose of the jars of flies. He had encountered Lily and Rudy there; they had asked what he was carrying. He had explained to them and had offered his treasure. It had been accepted with pleasure and had been the means of establishing a friendship on the instant. When he had left them to return to our third floor apartment, they were emptying the flies on the driveway and making plans about how best to use them.

I looked in from the porch to see if Mother appreciated his social advancement. Mother was staring at Father and he was shaking his head at her. Father said, "It's all right, Girl. We're living in a city now. Chances are we won't ever know the mothers and fathers of their friends. So let this stand for a beginning."

After that beginning, Brother played with Rudy and Lily every day. From a recluse he turned into a gadabout. His friends never came to our apartment, but Brother visited them in theirs so frequently that whenever he failed to be on hand at mealtime, mother would tap with the heel of a slipper on the radiator pipe of her bedroom, a signal to summon him if he were in the janitor's apartment, and he generally was. He said it was a lovely place, very cosy, and that Gus's wife, whose name was Mrs. Stonewall, gave him cookies. He was fond of her.

The next friends Brother met were two little English boys who came to spend the winter with their grandmother, Mrs. Benton. Mrs. Benton, with her two spinster daughters, lived in the old brick house next door on the south to our building. Brother and the two little boys met by talking to one another across the fence that separated the Bentons' beautiful big garden from our back yard.

Shortly after this opening gambit had been reported by Brother, Mrs. Benton came with her daughters to call on Mother. They were the first callers we had, though it was an event for which Brother and I had been in training ever since we had moved from the hotel to an apartment. Every afternoon when we went out to play Mother had reminded us that at a summons from her we were to come upstairs on the run, skim into clean clothes with the speed of a fireman hearing an alarm, and present ourselves, scrubbed, and with our best manners, at the door of the living room. Mother would then introduce us to the lady caller, or callers, and after that we would be asked to come to play with their children. This was the way in which our social introduction to Chicago would take place.

It had taken Mother a long time to realize that ladies coming into our apartment building during the afternoon were not coming to call on her. She expected that those she saw prefaced a ring at our doorbell and cards placed on the silver tray that stood waiting on the table in our front hall. She defended this belief by telling us, over and over, that in Muncie she had always called on newcomers to the church or neighborhood, and that furthermore, she was accustomed to believe that when someone came up the front steps of the dwelling in which you lived, that person was coming to see you.

When Mrs. Benton and her daughters did call, Mother was so astonished that she forgot to summon us, though Hilda had got us in from the back yard, into our clean clothes and posted in the hall outside the living room door, at a time record we had never equaled. The callers shook hands with us on their way out, and Mrs. Benton said she hoped that Brother would come to play with her grandsons.

Brother said that evening at supper how nice it was that he was making friends for Mother, too.

His own friendship with the Benton boys, however, became cemented by an overture on Brother's part, as remote from the customary pattern as his gift of flies to Rudy and Lily.

On his birthday he was allowed, even encouraged, to invite to a birthday supper his whole quiver of friends—the Benton boys, Lily and Rudy, and William Hart—and at the very opening of the meal he drew his assorted guests together by inquiring, "Do you want to know something about Chinese torture?"

Assured that they did, he continued, "Well, one way is, they can stretch your neck like this . . ."

He demonstrated by endeavoring to lift with both hands his head from the top of his neck. There was a loud crack and he gave a scream of pain. In no time at all the party was over, the guests dispersed, he was in bed and the doctor called. Brother was found actually to have put something out of place. He remained in bed, immobilized, for two weeks.

His absence, and the fact that they had never got round to the creamed chicken, let alone the birthday cake, caused Rudy and Lily to slack off in their relationship with Brother. William Hart's visits from the old neighborhood were very few anyway. The friendship between them was petering out from lack of proximity. But by the Chinese torture, Brother earned the devoted attention of the Benton boys. They came solicitously to see him every day while he was still bedded, and resumed active play with him the moment he was released. And they never failed to urge him to try another form of Chinese torture. Whenever I heard them playing in Brother's room, they were assuring him that they would like to see this "ever so."

Jack Stephens was the next to come into Brother's circle. His entry was by way of father's appendix.

Father came home from his office early one afternoon and told Mother that he had been seized with a pain so acute that he had finally been able to endure it only by bracing his knee against the edge of the desk and pressing it to his abdomen. When even that failed to give him relief, he had decided that he'd better come home. Mother put him to bed and telephoned at once for Dr. Black at the Del Prado. Dr. Black pronounced the ailment appendicitis, and said that Father must be taken at once to the hospital.

During the doctor's visit, I lurked in the doorway to the bedroom, edging as far in as I dared, and I heard Mother say that the thought of Father carted off to a strange hospital in a city overwhelmed her.

"If we were at home," she explained to Dr. Black, "we'd know every doctor in town, or even whom to call from Indianapolis. It's not that I don't trust a surgeon you would choose; it's only that I feel so lost here, so insignificant. In Muncie we were significant. That's an awful thing to say, but at a time like this, it helps. Father Kimbrough has been the head of the board of the hospital ever since it was built. Why I don't even know where a hospital is in Chicago. Couldn't we take Hal back to Muncie?"

Dr. Black told Mother he knew exactly how she felt, but that it was out of the question.

This conversation between Mother and the doctor took place in the bathroom adjoining Mother's and Father's bedroom. I heard it from the doorway, and I think Father did, too. He called from bed, "Girl, if Dr. Black is talking about taking me to a hospital, I want you to call Father Kimbrough. You're not to be saddled with this."

Mother called back to Father that they were coming right in, and added to Dr. Black, "I think that's a good idea. The only real friends we have here live across the hall from us. They come from Muncie but they're away. I'd at least like someone to know what's happening. If I call Father it won't hold up Hal's going, since you feel that's urgent, but at least it will be a comfort to know that we're not just slipping out of this apartment into thin air."

Dr. Black agreed, and they returned to the bedroom to talk it over with Father.

As soon as Dr. Black left, Mother telephoned Grandmother and Grandfather in Muncie. Grandfather's voice could be heard all over our apartment. He shouted that whatever the doctor's opinion was, Father was not to go to the hospital until he and Grandmother were there to see him and be with Mother. They would take the train that night and would be in Chicago at seven o'clock the following morning.

Mother protested that Dr. Black had stressed the urgency of an immediate operation. Grandfather's bellowed retort was, urgency or no urgency, no son of his was going to a hospital, particularly a city one, unattended. The doctor and Father's appendix would simply have to wait.

Mother hung up and reported this conversation to Father, though there was no need to. Father and I both had heard every word of it. His comment was that he wouldn't dream of ignoring his father's wishes, and that furthermore, he was not going to have Mother cope with a Chicago hospital by herself.

Mother telephoned Grandfather's decision to the doctor. Dr. Black tried to change the plan, but Father was adamant. So the hospital was called, the reservations and time of operation changed to the following day, and Father was packed in ice.

Grandmother and Grandfather arrived early the next

"My father's going to the hospital in an ambulance."

morning. While they were in Father's room, the door was closed. I couldn't hear anything in the hall, so I went out on the front porch. I was uneasy, but it was exciting to have Grandmother and Grandfather on an unexpected visit, and Father having something no one else in the family had ever had. I heard Brother's voice. I looked down and saw him sitting on the curb in front of our building.

A little boy was coming through the gate from his house across the street. When we had moved into the apartment his family had evidently been away, but we had seen the boy and his mother and father during the last week. Mother had asked Brother one night at supper if they had spoken to each other, and Brother said no, they hadn't. He'd been busy. Therefore, apparently what I heard Brother say was his way of introducing himself. He said, "My father's going to the hospital in an ambulance."

The little boy came immediately from his gate to the curb in front of his house.

"When's he going?" he asked.

Brother called back, "As soon as the ambulance comes."

From the little boy, "I have to go on an errand for my mother. Will it be here before I get back?"

From Brother, "Oh, no. It'll be a long time, I guess."

The little boy waved cordially.

"See you later," he said, and went off on a run.

Not five minutes after he had disappeared round the corner, the ambulance arrived. Father, rolled in blankets, was placed on the stretcher and carried down the three flights from our apartment, eased into the ambulance, and, with Mother, Grandmother and Grandfather beside him at their insistence, drove away.

Brother and I stood on the sidewalk and watched them out of sight. I was scared. I felt sick at my stomach, and completely left out of the family. I came back into the apartment and climbed the stairs, slowly, wondering whether I would throw up or not. Hilda, our maid, was going to take care of us and Mother was going to telephone from the hospital. But at the moment, none of that was any comfort to me.

In the apartment I went into the bathroom and tried throwing up, but I couldn't. Hilda was making Father's bed, and the sight of that scared me all over again. I went out quickly to the porch. I could see Brother sitting on the curb again, and at that minute, the little boy from across the street came around the corner toward his house, on the run, some packages in his arms.

Brother stood up and shouted, "It came, and it's gone. The ambulance took my father."

The little boy stopped in his tracks. He put down the packages very carefully at the gate. He didn't say a word, but he crossed the street, looking first to the left and right, and when he had come to where Brother was standing, he shot his fist out and punched Brother in the jaw. Brother was surprised, but flailed back, and they were at it, rolling on the ground, kicking and punching each other without a sound. I yelled to them to stop, but they paid not the slightest attention to me.

I ran into the house to get Hilda. I looked in every room for her. She didn't hear me calling. I found her on the back porch emptying the trash. By the time I got her out to the front porch, there was no one on the sidewalk below. But as we came back into the living room, Brother opened the front door, and walked in. His sailor blouse was in rags, he was streaked with dust and sweat, and there was a cut over his left eye that was bleeding. Before we could say anything, he stuck his thumbs under his arms, wagged his fingers, and said loudly, "We licked each other. He's my friend. His name is Jack Stephens. And he isn't mad at me any more. I promised that if Father died, and they brought him in a hearse, I'd let Jack know the very first one."

8. *Brother's Cultural Life*

WITH THE BROADENING OF BROTHER'S SOCIAL CONTACTS and the increase in his group activities, his cultural interest waned. This distressed Mother. She could not persuade him now to go with her to the Field Museum, nor the Art Institute, even with the lure of a possible moth or two on the steps of the Museum, and the certainty of a reward for pictures identified at the Art Institute.

He was engaged in a building operation in Jack Stephens' back yard. He did not wish to be diverted from it. He had, furthermore, increased his circle so that it now included Bill Kerr, Bob Le Tourneau and Bill Harpole.

Visiting Father in the hospital I reported to him the latest additions to Brother's set. Father was convalescing easily and uneventfully from his appendix operation, and was very much interested in everything going on at home during his absence. He was pleased, he said, at the way Brother was settling into the neighborhood, striking out and making friends. He was interested to know what overtures Brother had made to Jack Stephens to bring this about. I explained how Brother had offered to Jack the sight of an ambulance, and had then failed to come across, but that he had held out, to make up for his failure, the possibility of a hearse, with Father in it.

News of this had got around the neighborhood and the three latest additions to the circle had joined up, so as to be closely associated with him in the event that Father made good Brother's promise. Father was afraid, he said, that he was not going to be able to oblige, and that Brother was going to be in a tough spot. He advised Mother and me not to let Brother know the date of Father's homecoming, lest the sight of him, emerging under his own power from a vehicle, and that only a hired automobile, damage Brother both socially and physically.

Therefore Brother, coming home late one afternoon from his work at Jack Stephens', was surprised to find Father sitting in the living room, talking to Mother and me. Surprised and dismayed, though he tried not to show it. But he said, over and over, nervously, "I've got to tell the boys and Lily that you're home."

Father suggested that Brother keep it a secret until Father gave the word. When the doctor allowed him to walk up and down the stairs, he would accompany Brother to Jack Stephens' back yard, take a look at the construction under way there, and perhaps make some slight contribution to it. Would Brother consider that a good way to introduce him to his circle? Brother said heartily that it seemed to him an excellent idea and looked considerably relieved.

The first outing that Father took was to the Stephens' back yard, late one afternoon. I went with him, but mother said she had not met Mrs. Stephens and certainly did not wish to accomplish it by tramping into her back yard.

The whole circle was there, and they were building a shack of considerable size. Father introduced himself and everyone was surprised to learn who he was. They all looked at Brother, but Father said quickly that he had come over to make a little contribution to their building. It was a fine-looking structure, he said, and they were certainly using beautiful new lumber on it. He wanted to know if he might ask where they got it. Brother spoke up for them. They got it, he said, from a building that was being put up around the corner. Every night, before the group scattered, they took Jack Stephens' express wagon and piled it with all the lumber left over at the end of the day after the workmen had gone home. One of the boys added that it had been Brother's idea, and that it was certainly fine lumber.

Father agreed, and said that he would like to leave one dollar for the purchase of any extra nails or tools they might need. He suggested that Lily, as the only girl, act as treasurer so there would be no unfortunate discussion about who should take charge of it. Lily, who was Swedish and silent, smiled happily and grabbed it, stuffing it down the front of her middy blouse. The boys were pleased, and gave every evidence in their friendliness to Brother, that they considered the donation a reasonable exchange for a hearse. They were at work again when Father and I left.

On the way out of the yard, Father said he thought he had better see Mr. Stephens about a little problem in connection with the building. We rounded the corner of the house, went up the front steps and rang the doorbell. Mr. Stephens was at home, but Mrs. Stephens was out, he said. Father apologized for breaking in, as he called it, but explained why he had come over to see the building. Mr. Stephens agreed that it had been a critical situation for Brother.

"Now what I've discovered," Father continued, "is that those youngsters are swiping lumber from a construction job going on around the corner. But they don't know that they're swiping it. What my son has just explained to me is that every night after the workmen go home, the boys take the express wagon and gather up what, as they call it, is left over. Here's my predicament. If I point out that the lumber isn't left over, and that the gang is stealing, I'll then have to take steps about it—make them tear down the shack, return the wood—and you can see what a bad spot my son will be in once more. I've already given him one black eye by failing him on the hearse. I don't want to give him another. Under the circumstances I'd like to know how you'd feel about it if I saw the contractor of the new building, explained something of the situation to him and settled for whatever the boys have taken. It may not be the best way to teach the boys honesty, but I'll take that on later. Right now I'm concerned with helping my son to stay in right with his gang, after having knocked the props out from under him by my unfortunate recovery."

Mr. Stephens agreed with Father's idea. He had been away on a business trip, he explained, or he would have noticed the building in progress, and investigated the lumber. He thought it the luckiest thing in the world, he said, that he'd been away. But he insisted that Father allow him to share the expense.

After that, Mr. Stephens and Father met every morning on their way downtown and went around together to get from the contractor, the bill for the lumber taken by the boys the night before.

Father told Mother and me all about it and said that the contractor was very interested in the boys' enterprise. Mother said she hoped the boys weren't building anything dangerous, and Father laughed at her. But I'd been over a couple of times since my visit with Father, and I brought back the news that they were putting up a second floor. The second floor was also going to have a roof on top with an

opening to it. They had told me they were going to have
sentry duty up there.

Mother said anxiously, "Heavens! Why that will be a tall
building, not a shack."

I assured her that it wouldn't, because the first floor ceiling was so low you couldn't even stand up in the room; they
had to enter and remain at a crouch.

But a week later, Mother responded on the run to the
shouts from the gang assembled on the sidewalk below our
apartment, that Brother was hurt. She found him on the
ground in front of the shack just regaining consciousness.
He had been doing sentry duty on the roof, and had absent-
mindedly stepped back through the opening, but because
that one was not in line with the opening to the first floor,
instead of falling harmlessly to the ground, he had been
caught by the chin on the offset and knocked out cold.

That was when Mother insisted he must resume his cultural life, and forbade him to go back to shack construction.
She modified this dictum by inviting the group, with the
exception of Lily and Rudy, whose parents did not approve
of the theater, to a production in Chicago, of *Joseph and
His Brethren*. It had been widely advertised as a "magnificent spectacle" and Mother felt that since the theme was so
elevating, the entire occasion would be one that the children would remember.

She underestimated the memorable effect. Brother remembered it in nightmares for weeks, and after the performance itself, was in a condition of such shuddering horror, that he was unable to eat any supper and had to have
a light left on in his room before he would go to sleep. Even
then he awakened in the night with the first of the nightmares.

With ghoulish relish he shared with me the unforgettable

experience, by recounting how some thirty seconds after the curtain went up, a Nubian slave had dragged a beautiful fair-haired Christian across the stage, holding in his other hand a white-hot branding iron, and declaring that it was to be used to burn out her eyes. Immediately they had disappeared in the wings on the other side of the stage, her scream left the audience in no doubt that he had fulfilled his purpose.

I asked Mother, in Father's hearing, if this were true, and she admitted that it was, though she had thought she would not mention it. Father asked why she had not taken the little boys out, and she protested that to do such a thing seemed to her an extravagance we could not afford, since to take a whole group of children had cost considerably in the first place. Also she had reasoned that the play could not possibly contain anything worse; since it was bound to get better, the children would forget that early scene. She was mistaken, however, in this calculation. Shortly after the branding, Joseph was dragged onto the stage, as Brother described it to me, and thrust into a hole in the center of the floor. Over his cries of anguished protests, the top was sealed down.

After that some processions came and went; Brother was vague about this filling in. It had made very little impression on him. His attention was divided only between the wings from which the girl might reappear without her eyes, and the hole in the middle of the stage, where Joseph was sealed. The girl did not come back, but in the middle of the second act, the sealed chamber was opened, and Joseph dragged from it, a living skeleton. He had been young and handsome when they put him in, but this was fifty years later.

The other little boys were as impressed as Brother. Their mothers telephoned about it.

By leading the boys to culture, Mother did distract them, however, from the shack in Jack Stephens' back yard, and she boasted of that accomplishment to Father when Brother was out of hearing, but I was not. She was sure, too, she said, that the bad dreams at night would pass. Then she discovered that the memory of Joseph was being kept green by a game that Brother invented for the circle. The game was simple; it did not reveal Brother as a genius of originality or complicated design. It was simply a competitive experiment to determine what forms of physical hazard were feasible and not fatal.

Mother decided that the only way to efface the whole experience of *Joseph and His Brethren* was to plant another on top of it. So she took Brother and the little English boys to see Maude Adams in *Peter Pan*. This seemed to be an unqualified success. I went with them, but I sat on the other side of Mother, away from the boys, in order to dissociate myself from the distasteful company into which I had been forced. My immediate environment was the only flaw in the afternoon's entertainment. I was transported by the play, and the boys must have been to an even greater extent, because they sat still.

Mother reported all of this to Father with considerable satisfaction. Only good would come of this, she assured him, and happy memories.

Twenty-four hours later Brother introduced to the circle a flying game. The apartment building on the corner nearest us had instead of a back yard, a stone court. At some time a tenant had put up a rope swing between two of the several iron posts imbedded at intervals in the concrete for the purpose of holding clotheslines. The swing had worn out until there was left of it only a single strand with a big knot tied at the end.

Piecing together the details of the accident to the fat boy in that building, Mother and I found that the boys were willing and eager to give Brother the credit for using the strand of rope as an instrument for flying, and for padding the knot with burlap sacking, so that the flight could be accomplished in a sitting position. A flyer, boosted by the other boys, they explained, could shinny up one of the posts that supported the back porches of the two first-floor apartments, stand on the nearer porch railing holding on to the post until an assistant on the ground below swung the rope toward him. The rope never went the full distance to the porch railing. But when it got as close as was possible to send it, a flyer would let go the post, jump for the rope, grab it, and simultaneously assume a sitting position, like a fireman descending the pole. In this fashion, resting comfortably on the burlap padding, he achieved a tremendous sail through the air.

The fat boy was a stranger in the neighborhood. He had come on a visit to an aunt who lived in one of the apartments in that building. After watching from his aunt's back porch the flight achieved by every member of the circle during a considerable part of a Saturday morning, he announced his desire to enjoy one. Granted permission, an act of generosity on the part of the circle it was emphasized by each member when giving evidence, the boy refused all offers of detailed instruction. He had been watching them, he said, and he knew exactly what to do. He had, it turned out, mastered the technique, but had underestimated his bulk. This flaw in his calculations caused him to fall short of the rope when he jumped for

"Would you like to hear him again, hein?"

it from the railing, and to hit instead the stone courtyard in the sitting position of a fireman descending his pole.

His injury was not serious, but in order to plow under this association with Peter Pan, Mother took Brother to hear Pablo Casals. This could only produce an uplifting and, at the same time, a soothing effect, Mother assured Father and me. It could not inspire an aftermath of activity.

When they returned from this musical treat, Mother was in a glow of pleasure, bestowed almost evenly over Casals and Brother. Casals had been magnificent, she reported, and Brother, appreciating his superb artistry, had clapped wildly, and then feeling that insufficient, had stamped his feet. A gentleman sitting in the box next to theirs and separated from Brother only by the partition dividing the two boxes, had observed with pleasure Brother's enthusiasm. Only someone deprived of all his senses, Mother admitted, could have been unaware of it. Mother also deprecated the fact that she and Brother happened to have seats in a box, but had obeyed her feeling that if Brother's attention were to be held, he must be able to see as well as hear Casals play. She had been right in her feeling, she insisted in her report, not only because of Brother's enthusiasm, but because the gentleman in the next box, attracted by it, had leaned across the partition and said to Brother, "You would like to hear him again, *hein?*"

When Brother had asserted that he would like that very much, the gentleman had turned toward the stage, cupped his hands around his mouth and called loudly, "Pablo, encore."

Casals, hearing the voice above the applause had looked up, located it, smiled, bowed in that direction and given an encore.

"And who do you suppose," Mother concluded her recital to Father and me, "who do you suppose that gentleman was? Fritz Kreisler!"

For the next day or two Brother seemed to be under
the spell of music. He absented himself from the circle and
moved about in a kind of trance. During that period
Mother passed also into a cloud of dreams and telephoned
Lyon and Healey to find out how much a 'cello would cost.

This was followed by a week of absenteeism when his
whereabouts could not be tracked down, even by his circle.
The area permitted him to travel alone had been extended
over the passage of time since we had moved to Blackstone
Avenue, to a block in any direction from our building. A
generous radius, but one that was encompassed several
times over by the circle on a day's forays.

Father asked Brother at supper one night if Brother had
gone beyond his limit. Brother guaranteed he hadn't.
Father answered, "I believe you. But the boys and Lily tell
me they haven't been able to find you anywhere."

Brother said, "If you want to know, I'll tell you, only
I don't want my friends trailing me there."

Father assured him that he would keep the secret and that
Brother need not even tell it.

"I go to Mr. Harold Henry's apartment in the building
on the corner."

Mother interrupted him to say tremulously to Father
across the table, "Why, Hal, Harold Henry is a concert
pianist."

Later that evening, when Brother had gone to bed and
I was trying to read, she was picturing to Father their little
boy sitting on the dark steps in the hall outside Mr. Henry's
apartment, ear pressed against the door, listening to the

flood of glorious music within. The next day she engaged
Mr. Max Oberndorfer to give Brother piano lessons.

Brother showed no particular aptitude in this field except
for an uncanny ability to transpose to other keys any exercise or simple piece given him. This talent was only an
exasperation to Mr. Oberndorfer, so the lessons would
probably have petered out anyway, but they came to an
abrupt close because Hilda, our maid, threatened to leave.
The reason Hilda threatened to leave was that Brother had
begun to creep up on her, she said, and try to toss her over

his shoulder. Catching her this way unexpectedly, he had
very nearly succeeded once or twice. The surprise of it
displeased Hilda to the point of a contemplated departure.

Hilda was assured that she would not be crept up on
again, and Brother was asked to account for his extraor-
dinary behavior. He obliged reluctantly. He had made the
acquaintance of a Japanese who was houseman to Mr.
Harold Henry. This new friend was giving jujitsu lessons
to Brother in Mr. Henry's apartment, at such times as it
was unoccupied by Mr. Henry.

On this discovery of Brother's interest and talent, Mother
decided that piano lessons were a needless extravagance.
She reasoned further that plays and concerts had stimulated

more than his cultural advancement. With the purpose of retarding his growth in those auxiliary fields, she proposed also to save money, and with the money saved, send him to dancing class.

She sent him to a dancing class in the Fine Arts Building in town. The class was conducted by Mr. and Mrs. Bournique, both in their seventies, but adept together not only at teaching, but at demonstrating a waltz on the top of a piano stool. Mother had to accompany him every Friday afternoon to this class, not because of anxiety about his traveling there alone, but because without her he would remove the white gloves, Buster Brown collar, and the black silk stockings that were the accessory requirements of dancing class couture. In a telephone conversation when Mrs. Bournique reported Brother's eccentricities of apparel, and his tendency to desert his partner in the middle of a dance in order to swoop down upon an unwary couple and try out a bit of judo, she suggested firmly that Mother not only accompany him, but remain with him.

But Friday was the day on which the Chicago Symphony concerts took place, and the time of the concert and the dancing class overlapped. Mother submitted to this cutting short of her attendance at Orchestra Hall, but not for very long. The Friday afternoon concerts, she had said over and over to the family, more than made up for everything that moving from Muncie to Chicago had cost her. She could live happily all her days, a stranger in a city, so long as she had them. To give them up in order that Brother should keep on his Buster Brown collar, his white gloves and his long black silk stockings, was too much to ask, she announced to Father as he came in the door one afternoon, home from the office. Brother was not going to dancing school again until the next year, when he would be old enough for the Bourniques' intermediate class, held in the parish house of a church only a few blocks away. Coming down the hall to greet Father, I heard this announcement and turned on my heels instead, rushing back to the kitchen where Brother was, to tell him the news. He expressed his jubilant enthusiasm over it by throwing me.

Brother returned to life at the shack. His culture pattern dimmed for a while, but was revived by an invitation from the parents of the little English boys to go to a Saturday matinee at a theater. The parents, arriving to take their sons back to England, were spending a little time before their departure with Mrs. Benton, and had been told of Brother's theater parties. They wished, they said, to return the kindness. Mother was delighted for Brother to accept, and didn't even ask what they were planning to see, because, as she protested later to Father and me, "There is something about a British accent that is misleading. The English speak so beautifully they give the impression of having impeccable cultural taste. You feel abashed to question it."

Father said he didn't think it had been a question of taste, just ignorance. Whatever it was, it led them to take the boys to a performance of Nora Bayes and Jack Norworth in *The Sun Dodgers*. This provided the boys with a totally new field of inquiry and exploration. Told in song and story, the production made as deep a furrow in their memory as *Joseph and His Brethren*.

Not long after that Jack Stephens' uncle who had been a cowboy in the West, took over the entertainment of Jack and Brother when the Stephenses and the Kimbroughs were, separately, away for a week end. The little boys were left in the charge of the maid in each household. On Saturday afternoon, Jack's uncle took them to a vaudeville show at the Palace. One of the star performers was a young woman who sang "Oh, You Beautiful Doll" and invited volunteers from the audience to come up and join her. Jack's uncle complied. On Saturday night he took the boys to see the six-day bicycle races in the amphitheater of the stockyards. They came home at four in the morning.

Brother told us about his week end at breakfast on Monday. He had never in his entire life, he said, had such a thoroughly satisfactory time, nor seen anything so beautiful as the act at the Palace.

Mother let this stand for some time as the peak of Brother's cultural progress. She explained this to Brother.

"I think," she said, "we'll let things just settle for a while."

9. Brother's Financial Life

SHORTLY AFTER BROTHER ENTERED THE FIRST GRADE AT THE Kenwood Public School, he fell in love with his teacher, Miss Wood. His feeling for her was not sullied by any thought of gain. It was a pure, clear flame of devotion and service. When at the end of the year he found that he had achieved promotion to the second grade, and that this accomplishment involved being separated from her, he was distracted with grief. He told both her and the family no one could make him learn any more, if he didn't want to; given the choice between education and Miss Wood, he preferred Miss Wood. There he would stay.

Inexorably moved forward, however, when the autumn term of the second year began, he took his place in the room adjoining Miss Wood's, but announced with sullen fervor he was not going to like it.

Perhaps it was this forceful separation that tarnished the purity he had heretofore displayed in his approach to love. When his emotional interest was provoked again, it was by a classmate in the second grade. And this time it was not love for love. The little girl's name was Verjean, and her father was an army officer who had brought back from the Philippines a collection of bolo knives. Brother's attraction to Verjean herself was so short-lived as to last only for one afternoon. But during that time when he went to her house to play after school, he saw the collection of knives. The difficulty that presented itself immediately to him was that though by the end of the afternoon he was bored by the company of Verjean, and wanted with all his heart to return to his circle, he had not lost interest in the knives. He wanted very much to see them again without undergoing the tedium of Verjean's society.

He achieved this, and made money at the same time. By this achievement, too, he was back on base again, immersed in his two sound and absorbing interests—things to look at, and money—a little ashamed that he had ever strayed from them.

Our parents knew about the affair Wood. It had taken the persuasion and authority of both of them to separate him from her. But the Verjean flurry was revealed to us in snatches, during a very severe digestive upheaval that followed his combined money-making and knife-viewing scheme.

He had gone to friends of his, the Mantia Brothers, who owned a grocery store where Mother was a regular customer. Learning from them that Verjean's mother also patronized that establishment, he had offered to deliver groceries after school, provided that the supplies for her family were included in his allotment. He figured that entering by way of the kitchen, he could slip into the den and look over the knives, untrammeled by the companionship of Verjean—this pleasure to be further enhanced by a remuneration from the Mantia Brothers.

The scheme had worked to Brother's and the Mantias' full satisfaction. They assured Mother afterward he had been a conscientious worker, even taking on loads for delivery to third- and fourth-floor apartments that the brothers considered far too heavy for him to carry. They had hoped he would work for them a long time. They lost him, however, and Mr. and Mrs. Kimbrough very nearly lost their son.

No one in the family had known that Brother was delivering groceries. Even Hilda, whose eye and ear were always alert to Brother's and my activities, had thought he was playing every afternoon at the shack. But one night he awakened us all by an attack of such severity that Dr. Black was sent for. Trying to learn if Brother had taken poison, since the spasms were so violent, Dr. Black drew from him the story of Verjean, the knives, the business association with the Mantia Brothers, and the additional disclosure of a daily snack pressed upon him by his generous employers. This snack, at the end of the day, had consisted of a loaf of bread cut in half, and the center hollowed out. The hollow had then been filled with alternate layers of Bermuda onions and salami. His appetite for supper had not been impaired by this, perhaps because Mother sternly restricted our evening meal to very limited and simple fare, believing that it was not healthful for children to go to bed immediately after a heavy meal. This was probably the reason why Brother's digestive system was not tuned to a luxurious Italian diet.

After Brother's recovery, he was forbidden to engage in any occupation that offered remuneration without first getting permission from Mother and Father. To soothe his anguished protests at being deprived of money and also to insure comparative peace of mind by knowing his whereabouts on a Saturday afternoon, Mother allowed him to go with his friends to the movies. She disapproved strongly of this form of entertainment. I knew this, and when I questioned her vehemently about her lenience, since she was inexorable about not permitting me to go, she admitted that it was because if he were not there he would be thinking up things to do beyond the realm of her imagination to forestall.

She could scarcely forbid me, however, to go to pictures Brother was permitted to attend, and so I went to a few of the Saturday matinees of which he and his friends were earnest and constant patrons. Arriving at the theater I sat as far from Brother and his group as possible. In a short time, however, I ceased demonstrating my victory over Mother, because neither the audience nor the program was to my liking.

The Picture Palace was on Fifty-first Street, and the afternoon session began at one o'clock. It included a serial, *Bronco Billy Anderson*, and a comedy series, starring a gentleman called Musty Suffer. A Pathe News was thrown in to give the patrons their ten cents worth. The patrons were always noisy, but when they grew threateningly obstreperous, the operator would turn off the picture until they quieted down. Frequently the film would break, and when that happened, a sign reading "Just a minute, please" would be flashed on the screen. The pianist who played appropriate music throughout the showing of all the pictures, would strike up a familiar melody, and the patrons would sing in unison until the film was repaired.

Mother commenced to feel that there was a justification for the motion picture industry, and she told Father and me so when we went for a walk one Saturday afternoon. She knew exactly where Brother was at that moment, she explained, and furthermore, his sustained interest in Bronco Billy had evidently pushed from his mind schemes for making money.

It was only two days after this conversation took place when, on a Monday noon, Brother, returning from school, met the members of a steamroller crew, engaged to resurface the street in our block. He was thereupon late getting home, and tardy at the afternoon session of school, but by suppertime he knew the names and was a friend of every man in the outfit. He told us about all of them at the table.

The next night he announced, as we sat down to supper, he had found a way to earn a little money. Father observed to Mother across the table that perhaps she had spoken a little too soon in praise of the motion picture industry. Mother's retort was to promise that she was going to ally herself the following day with a committee then being formed to abolish motion pictures for children. Brother, annoyed by the interruption, asked if he could tell them his idea for earning money. Reminded by Father that he would have to tell and get permission before taking one step toward carrying it out, Brother answered that all he wanted was a chance to tell, and disclosed his idea.

Talking things over with the men, he said, he had discovered that they brought coffee and milk along with their dinner pails, but that they couldn't keep the coffee hot, nor the milk cold. The idea had then struck Brother that he could start out for school a little earlier in the morning, go over to the steamroller, get the day's milk the crew had brought, and bring it back upstairs to our apartment for Hilda to keep in the ice-box. Then at noon, on his way home, he'd pick up their containers of coffee, bring them upstairs for Hilda to heat on the stove, and return them, piping hot, for the men's dinner. For this, he had estimated, he ought to be paid five cents a week.

Mother and Father told him they would let him know their decision the next morning, and sent him off to bed.

I heard them talking it over that evening while I was doing my lessons. Father said he liked to see this enterprise in the boy and hated to have it discouraged. Mother agreed with him but added that she would be only too ready to encourage it if she could ever be sure that Brother's line of activity would not deviate from his purpose. In almost every undertaking of his, however, financial or recreational, the plan was acceptable, but the fulfillment unexpected. They could think of nothing about this transaction that could bounce back at them with a surprise, and so the next morning they gave Brother permission to work for the construction gang.

Brother went on the payroll that very day, and nothing unexpected occurred. Even Hilda was co-operative; she cooled the milk and heated the coffee without protest. By the end of the week Mother had ceased to be anxious, and Father admitted that he had told some of the men going into town on the Illinois Central train with him in the morning about his son's business initiative.

At supper the night before Thanksgiving, Father remarked to Brother that he guessed Brother wouldn't be working the following day since it was a holiday. Brother answered quickly that he'd asked about that and the men had told him they were going to work—it was a rush job. Mother said she thought that very hard on the men and on the families of the men, not to be able to have a Thanksgiving dinner. She considered, she added, Thanksgiving one of the happiest family occasions of the year. Father told her not to be too sorry for the men; they probably would enjoy getting paid that day just as much as a piece of turkey. Mother insisted this was a low point of view and one to be deplored; the men, she asserted, ought to have both pay and turkey.

That was the end of the conversation on the subject.

The next day at noon, while Mother, Father and I were waiting in the living room for Hilda to announce dinner, Father asked where Brother was, and Mother told him Brother had gone down to get the steamroller crew's coffee and bring it up to be heated.

At that moment the front doorbell rang. Mother jumped nervously, and asked who on earth could be coming to see us at that hour? Father went out into the front hall and opened the door.

Brother stood in the doorway, surrounded by the steamroller crew. Brother was beaming.

"Father," he said, "these are my friends, that I told you about. I said you and Mother wanted them to have turkey dinner as well as their pay, so would they come up and have ours with us? Here they are."

Mother had risen from her chair somewhat unsteadily, but she came into the hall and joined Father. I followed her. Brother introduced each of his friends by name, and we shook hands all around.

The turkey was considerably stretched, but Father made it go round, by slicing it thin and making sandwiches from it for our guests. They didn't want to come into the dining room, so they ate in the living room, and Brother with them. Mother's, Father's and my meal was skimpy, but Brother said afterward theirs had been fine, and each of the guests when he left assured mother it had been a high-class meal.

We didn't entertain them again, but Brother continued his employment. Mother's anxiety, however, had been quickened, and she took to ordering extra provisions daily, until the steamroller moved out of our neighborhood.

Brother's next source of revenue was St. Paul's Episcopal Church, a block away from our apartment. Mr. Richardson was the choirmaster there, and a distinguished musician. He was Welsh, small and light in build, with black hair and a pale complexion. Very high-strung, he was frequently irascible, and always intolerant of any obstacle to his forming the best possible choir. He was, therefore, allowed to make up its body from whatever sources he chose, and since a voice and a good ear were his only requisites for membership, he was indifferent to the religious background of his group. He kept in touch with the music teachers and school teachers in the neighborhood in order to spot a possible candidate. Brother's teacher recommended Brother. Mr. Richardson sent for him, gave him a trial and accepted him. He took in at the same time a classmate of Brother's, whose name was Irving Epstein.

Brother brought the news of his admission to the supper table that night. He was more excited than I had ever seen him. The reason for this turned out to be that choirboys were paid fifty cents a month, a wage scale Brother had not known existed. Mother approved the employment immediately. Father was dubious. We were Presbyterians, and Father was not sure, he said, that he wanted Brother involved in the trappings of the Episcopal Church. But Mother reminded him of their agreement that Brother and I should be allowed to make our own choice of denomination. Father conceded the agreement, but demurred at this way of making use of it. At the time he had entered into this understanding with Mother, he said, he had not anticipated that a selection would be motivated by fifty cents a month. Mother's answer to this was that with or without the fifty cents, Brother would be given an opportunity to learn intimately the Episcopal service and doctrine, and at the same time acquire a remarkable musical training not available in the Presbyterian Church. Brother volunteered that they didn't pay fifty cents, either, in the Presbyterian Church.

Father gave in.

It was not long before we were all going to St. Paul's Church, partly because of its beautiful music, and partly to keep an eye on Brother. Mr. Richardson was a friend of Aunt Nelle and Uncle Channing Ward, who lived across the hall from us. Richy, as the choirboys called him, would come over to the Wards to play two-piano music with Aunt Nelle, and my family would slip across the hall to hear it.

When Richy told Mother that she might come to his choir rehearsals if she liked, and bring me occasionally, she was enormously flattered, because he never allowed the choir mothers to be there. "Not a musician among them," he declared.

Rehearsals were held in a basement room of the parish house. Richy conducted with a baton made from half a broomstick. He also used it to poke the stomach of a boy singing off pitch. At the beginning of a rehearsal he always took his watch from his pocket, and laid it on the top of the piano. One evening, when Mother and I were listening, he became exasperated at a lagging tempo in the Stainer "Crucifixion," and crashed the broomstick down on the piano, and on the watch. The air was filled with flying springs, screws, and other mechanical inwards. Brother earned five cents that night by staying after rehearsal to pick up every tiny piece.

With Brother's admission to the choir, I found church-going more interesting than it had been before. I accompanied Mother and Father every Sunday without much protest. I would listen with excited apprehension for the processional, knowing that because it was begun in the robing room just underneath the organ with the door closed, the boys had to sing it a half tone lower than the organ was playing, in order to synchronize, at that distance, with the instrument. But as the choir emerged into the church proper, the pitch had to be lifted a half tone on exactly the note reached as the door opened. If there was any hitch, a terrifying scene with Richy would follow the service. That was also interesting to anticipate. When the anthem came, I would remember how at rehearsal Richy, after starting them on it, would walk out of the rehearsal room, through the basement, up the stairs, around the first floor of the parish house, down the stairs and back to the rehearsal room. He did this to test the pitch. If they were off, he would bellow at them from whatever part of the building he was in, and they would have to start again.

Brother enjoyed weddings and funerals more than regular Sunday services, because participation in those special events netted each choirboy a dollar. He had no preference; a funeral was just as enjoyable as a wedding. Actually, funerals, he admitted, had a little the edge on weddings, because there were more of them. He developed a ghoulish interest in obituary notices, running his finger down them on the page, to see if any of the deceased listed were members of St. Paul's parish.

The year a blizzard nearly paralyzed the whole city, and all schools were closed for two weeks because coal couldn't be delivered to keep the fires going, Brother crawled on his hands and knees to vesper services on two succeeding Sundays. Mother was terrified to have him go, but he had protested so at failing Richy that she gave in. When he came back from each of these, he reported that there had not been absent one member of the choir, but at one of these services, there had been only three people in the congregation.

By Christmas week that year, the weather had softened; the streets and sidewalks had cleared, people were moving about again, though I walked to school between banks of snow on either side of me higher than my head. In the yard of the Kenwood School there was a drift up to the second-story windows.

Mr. Richardson was working the boys furiously for the Christmas Eve Midnight Watch Service, one of the most beautiful of the year. So many people came, the church was always packed to the doors. I was allowed to stay up for it inasmuch as my young brother sang in it, as I had pointed out to the family indignantly, when the question had first arisen.

That night we left particularly early in order to be sure of sitting in our pew. The sky was clear, the air cold but dry. The banks of snow on either side of us were tall shadows. Mother said softly over her shoulder to Father and me as we followed her, single file, that this was just the way a Christmas Eve should be—still and beautiful and cold. She thought we would remember it.

For this service only candles were used in the church, and when we came up the aisle to our pew, an altar boy was lighting the last of them with a long taper. The light from the candles was soft and uneven; it was not easy to see clearly into the choir stall, but when the organ music began, Mother whispered across me to Father that Mr. Richardson wasn't playing.

"The music is so difficult this year," she said, "he probably doesn't trust the boys to start without him."

The church filled up. People came in blowing a little because they were out of breath from the cold, and there was more rustling than usual while extra layers of coats and scarves were taken off in the warm church.

Mother said this was just the way a Christmas Eve should be.

When the first words of the processional sounded faintly from the robing room, the rustling stopped. There were no sounds but the organ softened to a whisper, and the far-off high voices, like small and distant bells. And then the door opened, the boys came into view, the music swelled until all the church was drenched in the beat and the sound.

The processional ended with each boy at his place. When they were seated, they remained quiet, no boy looking at

another, no fiddling nor usual restless squirming, everyone looking straight ahead of him. And this was so unusual I whispered to mother, "Richy has them scared tonight, all right."

They rose again for the anthem, and moved flawlessly into the opening note. When Bradley Davis, who was eleven, took the first note of his solo, his high, sweet, skylark voice was exactly true. Not long after this opening, I could see even in the wavering candlelight that he was crying. I nudged Father and indicated it in pantomime. I was astonished. Father nodded that he saw it, too. We both turned to Mother and saw that she was in tears herself. She managed to whisper, "It's so beautiful. The boys themselves are aware of it."

Little by little I could see tears rolling down the face of every boy.

The service ended. The choir filed out singing the recessional, and after it, in the room below stairs, the sevenfold amen, sure and steady in pitch, for all its difficult and interwoven pattern. When the last amen had faded out and we had risen from our knees, Mother said with a catch in her voice, "That's the most beautiful Midnight Watch I have ever heard."

We came outside and saw Brother waiting a few feet away from the doorway. The moment he caught sight of Mother, he flung himself at her, pushing his way through groups of people in his path. He buried his face against her and burst into racking sobs. I had very seldom in my life seen Brother cry at all, and this uncontrollable weeping was horrifying. Mother bent over him and pulled his head away from her coat, holding it between her hands. She stooped down and said,

"What is it, darling? What's the matter?"

And finally Brother was able to answer.

"He's dead. Richy's dead. In the rehearsal room. He stuffed up all the cracks and turned on the gas."

At Brother's first words, everyone within hearing seemed instantly turned to ice. There was not the squeak of a footstep on the snow. I could have counted to ten before anyone spoke. Then sharp voices cracked the silence.

"What did he say?"

"Richy's dead?"

"What's that?"

Mother had her arm around Brother. I could feel him

shaking when I reached out to pat him dumbly. Father said, "Go on home, Girl," and went back into the church. I saw other men move from the clumps of people to the lighted doorway and disappear inside.

Little boys came running toward us from the side door that the choir used. They were all clamoring words like,

"He killed himself tonight."

"Before the service."

"They only found out when it was time for him to play the organ."

And one voice so high and shrill it must have come from Bradley Davis who had sung the solo, "But we did the service for him, and we didn't go off pitch."

The choir sang at his funeral.

That evening Brother said he didn't want any supper, could he be excused? He had an errand to do. Mother said, yes, he could, but she would like to know where he was going.

"I'm going to the church," he said, "so I can put the dollar I got for today in the collection box for the poor. I don't want it, and I'm not going to sing in the choir any more."

10. Opening Day

MY FIRST DAY AT MISS FAULKNER'S SCHOOL WAS FULL OF surprises. I had thought it was going to be like Miss Richey's in Muncie. Miss Richey's School was at the Frank Ball's house. Every morning we had had opening exercises on the stair landing in the house and after that, lessons in the children's playhouse. When Mother had taken me to see Miss Faulkner a week before the term began, the first thing I'd noticed was that her school was in a house, too. We'd opened an iron gate, gone up some steps to a front porch, and Mother had rung the bell. A colored butler had opened the door and shown us into a parlor on the left of a center hall.

Miss Faulkner had come in before I'd had time to look around, but when she had finished talking to Mother, I'd asked whose house her school was in. She'd said it was her family's house; her parents lived there, her sister Georgene, who was head of the kindergarten, Miss Anne Shaw, who was going to teach me music appreciation, and Miss Sarah, who had charge of the housekeeping. She was Miss Elizabeth, she'd explained, and the head of the school. She'd asked me questions then about Miss Richey's School and had taken us across the hall to a long room like the parlor

except that there were blackboards on the wall and no furniture. This was going to be my classroom, she'd said, and
added that the desks had been taken out for the summer for
repainting but would be back before school opened. Sixth,
seventh, and eighth grades were in this room. Mother had
suggested that we shouldn't take any more of Miss Faulkner's time to show me the rest of the school since Mother
had seen it and I would soon be familiar with it. She knew
how busy Miss Faulkner must be. I'd thought Mother must
mean the rest of the house. It hadn't occurred to me that
there would be more of the school than this room, and I
hadn't been interested in seeing a house. We'd said good-by
to Miss Faulkner and the butler had opened the front door
for us.

At breakfast on the day school opened, I asked Mother if
she would walk there with me. She said she thought it was
better for me to go alone; the school was only three blocks
from home, I knew my way, and I would meet the girls
more easily if I arrived without my mother. I had no
qualms about arriving. I could hardly wait to meet the ten
or twelve children that would be there—that was the number of us at Miss Richey's—and by afternoon I would have
friends in Chicago. We would go to each other's house to
play. It would be just like Muncie.

The reason I didn't want to walk to school by myself was
something different. I wasn't scared, but even when I knew
exactly where I was, I felt as if I were lost because nobody
that I passed knew who I was. In Muncie when I walked
downtown on an errand for Mother, everybody I passed, or
nearly everybody, said hello, and if they didn't call me by
name, said something like, "Hal Kimbrough's little girl,
aren't you?" Or, "Now let me see. Whose child are you?"

And when I told them, they said, "Of course. I might have known. Kimbrough all over."

I didn't know everybody in Muncie who spoke to me. Adults never seemed to expect children to know them, but they knew me. In Chicago nobody had ever asked me whose daughter I was. Sometimes I had wanted to stop the person passing me and say, "Do you know what my father's name is?"

I never did this, of course. I made up a game instead that was to walk close to the buildings, with my head down, and play a down scale with my right hand, along the stone of the building. The game was that, since you weren't looking, you couldn't tell when you came to the corner of the building and the street, and you had to stretch your fingers around the corner, put your third or fourth finger over your thumb, just as if you were playing a scale, and get it around the corner. If you could do that, then you could look up and cross the street or turn the other way—do whatever you had to do. But if the fingering wasn't right at the corner, you had to go back to the beginning of the building and start again. Once I had come around a corner with my fingering just right and my head down, but I'd butted into a woman coming from the other direction and hugging the building because the day was windy. She had said, "What on earth do you think you're doing?"

That was the only time a passer-by had ever spoken to me.

Going to school the first day, I passed a great many people on their way to the Illinois Central Station to go downtown to work and children on their way to the Kenwood Public School. Nobody spoke to me, of course, and I felt the edges of panic, but I thought about the new friends waiting for me at Miss Faulkner's, and I didn't run back home.

When I went up the front steps at the school and rang

the bell, the colored butler who, the week before, had shown Mother and me in, was at the door, but he didn't show me in. He said, "This is the family entrance. The school entrance is around the corner," and shut the door.

I went back down the steps and to the corner where I stood a few minutes. There was an entrance that seemed to go into the side of the house, but I thought it must be another building stuck up against the Faulkner house, the way apartment buildings were in Chicago. Crowds of children were shoving and pushing into it. This was nothing like Miss Richey's School. I was sure it was a public school next door, but finally I walked near enough to a bunch of girls to ask, "Is this the entrance to Miss Faulkner's School?"

They answered things like, "That's right," and, "It certainly is. That's what it isn't nothing else but." And they pushed on in.

I tried to decide that it would be all right for me to go home, but Mother had said when I left what she always said every morning when I went to school, "Remember—with your shield or on it."

So I walked through the entrance.

I came into the school at the far end of a hall. I could see on my right the front door where Mother and I had come in. I couldn't see it immediately because there were so many girls in my way, all calling to other girls and saying had they had a nice summer, yes, wonderful, peachy. As soon as I did see the front door, I knew that my school was across the hall from where I was standing, and little by little I pushed through to that room. A lady holding a long sheet of paper in her hand stood in the doorway. She was tiny, with beautiful fluffy blonde hair piled on her head, though I didn't notice that for the first minute or two, nor hear her speak to me, because I couldn't believe my eyes. There were rows of desks, in pairs, down the whole room that had been empty the week before. There was a center aisle between, but I knew there must be at least forty desks—forty children in my school. We'd be there all night, I thought, reciting one at a time the way we had done at Miss Richey's. Or would we recite in pairs, like the way the desks were arranged?

The lady at the door was speaking to me, I realized, and I pulled my eyes away from all the desks to look at her. I saw her blonde fluffy hair and her very blue eyes that almost closed when she smiled. She was smiling. She said, "I've been asking you to tell me your name. Mine is Miss Farr, and this is my room. I think you belong here, don't you?"

I told her my name and said I thought I did belong here because it was where Miss Faulkner had brought Mother and me the other day.

Miss Farr said that was right and put a check beside my name on the long sheet of paper she was holding. She pointed to a pair of desks, and told me that was where I was going to sit, but my seatmate wasn't coming for another week. She didn't say what my seatmate's name was because other girls were crowding around her, hugging her or shaking hands, and she told me the name of some of them. I didn't hear them in the noise, and the girls didn't pay any attention to me, so I went over to the desk Miss Farr had pointed out and sat down at it.

A bell rang in the hall, and all the girls out there rushed into the room, squealing about where their desks were and who was paired with whom. A second bell rang and everybody was quiet at once. Miss Farr conducted morning exercises, and they were almost exactly like Miss Richey's, so for a few minutes I knew what was going on.

But the minute the exercises were over, Miss Farr asked

two girls who sat in the front row to distribute our schedules and gave them piles of stiff, large cards that had been
stacked on her desk. Every schedule had a name on it, and
the girls knew almost every one of them. When one of them
didn't, she would call the name and the new girl would put
up her hand or say, "Here." Gretchen Harbach, Josephine
Root, Clara Cary, Marguerite Fellows were some of the
names I heard, and I said them over to myself to remember
for when we got to be friends. But the girl who had my
card said, "Emily Kimbrugg?" and made a funny face.
Everybody screamed. I didn't say Kimbrough because it
was so awful to have everybody turn around to look at me.
I put up my hand, and as soon as I got it, I looked hard at
my card because I didn't know what else to do. I couldn't
make any sense out of it, however, no matter how hard I
looked. It said things like, "English, 2; History, 5; Arithmetic, 1; Recess; Music; French, 6; Latin, 7." And in another
column, "8:50, 9:30, 10:10, 10:50, 11:40, 12:20.

Miss Farr was speaking again, and I paid attention to her,
though I still looked at my card in case anyone was still
looking at me. She was saying to fasten our schedules on
the cover of one of our big notebooks so that we would
always have the schedule with us. We would find the notebooks in our desks and also some of our new books. Would
we please take out our new books quietly and go over them
to acquaint ourselves with the general outline of work for
the year? Also, would we study our schedules, please, very
carefully?

I got out my books and pasted my schedule on the cover
of a notebook, using paper rings that had glue on one side
—we'd had those at Miss Richey's. I opened the books, one
by one, and looked through them. Then I tried to study my
schedule, but I couldn't make any sense out of it at all. So
I decided that I'd done as much as I was expected to do.

I got up from my desk and left the room. I looked around the hall a little, and then I went outside. The grounds weren't anywhere near so big as at the Ball's: I could see the whole of them from one spot. So I went through the gate and out on the street. I walked down to Forty-seventh Street, not disturbed by the people who passed me because I was miserable anyway about the number of strange people in the school that I had thought was going to have only twelve pupils.

Forty-seventh Street was a busy thoroughfare with a trolley-car line and shops. I looked in the shop windows, watched a streetcar unload at the end of the line and the conductor switch the overhead trolley for the return trip, and then I walked back to the school the way I had come. I had not been gone more than half an hour, but Miss Farr was out on the front steps of the school. Miss Faulkner was with her, both talking to a policeman. When they heard me shut the gate, they all wheeled around and looked at me. Miss Farr and Miss Faulkner began to ask me questions as I came up the walk. Was I all right? Where had I been? Why had I gone outside? Had anybody coaxed me off the grounds? I thought I had never heard anything so silly, but I didn't say so. I answered their questions and explained that at Miss Richey's we always went outside on nice days when we had finished what we had been asked to do. I had finished looking over my new books inside of two or three minutes so I had gone out.

The policeman said, "Well, everything seems to be all right around here now so I'll be moving along."

Miss Farr and Miss Faulkner thanked him for coming and said they were sorry to have put him to any trouble.

"That's what we're for," he answered. "No trouble at all, and I'm glad there wasn't any for the little girl." He went off down the walk.

Miss Faulkner and Miss Farr walked back into the school on either side of me. They explained that I could not go for a walk even if I had finished my work. The most surprising thing of all was that they said I could not go anywhere except to the bathroom without asking permission. They also told me that I had given them great concern. When Miss Farr had realized that I was gone longer than necessary for a trip to the bathroom, she had left the room herself to look for me and finally had called Miss Faulkner. When they'd been unable to find me, they had telephoned Mother. She should be arriving at any minute. Miss Faulkner had also telephoned the police station and was just giving a description of me to the officer, she said, when I'd walked through the gate.

"You see, Emily," she added, "this is not Muncie. Things can happen in a city to a little girl."

As if I didn't know that, I thought. Things were happening to me every minute in a city: forty children or more in a school, a policeman called because you went for a walk, Mother sent for, schedules, big notebooks—and then to tell me this wasn't like Muncie.

Miss Faulkner said that she would speak to Mother when she came; there was no need to bring me out of class.

Miss Farr went into the schoolroom with me, but there was nobody there. This was a surprise to me, too.

Miss Farr asked to see my schedule.

"Let's see where you're supposed to be," she said.

I thought I was supposed to be in school since I wasn't supposed to be taking a walk, but I got out of my desk my notebook with the schedule on it and handed it to her. She ran a pencil down the little squares on it.

"English," she said, "in the dining room, with Mrs. Rogers."

She took me across the hall to a room behind the parlor and opened the door.

"Mrs. Rogers," she said, "this is Emily Kimbrough. She was detained. She is not to be counted tardy. I'll explain it to you later."

Mrs. Rogers smiled kindly at me. I liked the way she looked. She had brown hair, parted in the middle, and nice eyes. There were about twelve girls in the room. Some of them had sat near me in the other schoolroom that I had thought until now was the only schoolroom. The girls looked at me and at one another. I knew they were curious about where I had been, but I made up my mind not to tell them if they should ask me after class.

Mrs. Rogers put sentences on the blackboard and underneath put the same words on lines, some going across the board, some slanting down from the words going across. She called this doing something to a sentence, but I didn't know what she was talking about. She asked if there were any questions, but the only one I wanted to ask was, "What are you talking about?"

So I didn't say anything.

Presently a bell rang, and all the girls jumped up. Mrs. Rogers said she would tell me where to go if I would show her my schedule and that one of the girls would take me. One of the girls did take me. Her name was Virginia Cornwall, she said. She took me upstairs to a small room and introduced me to Miss Osgood, the History teacher. Miss Osgood was tall and thin. Her hands were big, the fingers bent back when she stretched them out, and her fingernails were cut very short. When she wrote on the blackboard, she used a very small piece of chalk and put all her fingers around it, close to the writing end. I looked away from her because I was afraid all her fingers were going to scrape on the board. I put my tongue between my teeth, too, so that if she did scrape, the sound wouldn't hurt so much. Even though I didn't look, I listened a little to what Miss Osgood said, but I didn't understand much of it.

Through the open door of our classroom I could see across the hall a room as big as the one downstairs that I had thought was our whole school. Older girls than those in my class were sitting at desks there. On the way out of History I asked Virginia what it was, and she told me that was the Academic department, where the older girls belonged. Ours was the Intermediate department. I asked if there were more besides, and she said, oh, yes, the Primary and the kindergarten. I was very surprised.

Back downstairs for Arithmetic with Miss Farr. I didn't understand anything she said, but she wrote on the blackboard with a long piece of chalk and held her fingers back from the writing end so I watched her. I was glad to see her again. When Arithmetic period was over, she asked how I was getting on with my schedule, was there anything about it I wanted to ask her? I wanted to tell her that I thought the whole thing the most confusing I had ever run up against, but I only asked her what the numbers on it meant. The number of the room, she told me, and the time I was due there. Each room had a number on the door except the one to which I was to go after recess, the third-floor hall for Music Appreciation, and after that Ear Training, both in the same place. The period, she said, was divided in halves, with two teachers, Miss Anne Shaw Faulkner for Appreciation and Mr. Oberndorfer for Ear Training. I was surprised to find that we were going to stay in one spot for two classes, but I wasn't surprised to learn that we were to be mixed up by having two teachers in one period.

At recess we were given cocoa and crackers in the dining

room. An old woman ladled it out of a pot, the tiniest
woman and the biggest pot I had ever seen. Before she
served it, she beat and beat it with an egg beater until foam
blew up high over the top. She held her arms as high as her
head to turn the egg beater. She had very brown skin, criss-
crossed with wrinkles, and sharp, brown eyes. I wanted
foam in my cup, but the girls who had been there longer
than I kept pushing me out of the way. Virginia stopped a
minute to talk to me. I asked her who the old woman was,
and she told me her name was Barby, that she had come
from England when she was fourteen and been Mrs. Faulkner's maid for over fifty years. By the time I reached Barby
all the foam was gone, and I had plain cocoa with crackers.
When I finished it, I went back to my room and sat at my
desk until the bell rang because I felt silly standing around
by myself.

The classroom on the third floor was the center hall,
equipped with a piano, blackboard, and chairs. The closed
doors all around it were to the Faulkner bedrooms, Virginia whispered, but no one ever saw the doors open. Some
of the girls thought there was probably something awful in
them and were scared to come up here. I shuddered and
moved with her to a place near the stairs so that we could
rush down if anything awful should come out.

Miss Anne Shaw was larger than the other teachers, and
her hair looked as if it didn't have enough hairpins in it. I
watched it at first to see if it would fall down, and then I
realized that she wasn't bothering about saying over our
names to see who was there. She was starting right in to talk
about the instruments of an orchestra. She asked how many
of us expected to go to the Chicago Symphony that year,
and I said I did. I said Father had been able to get two tickets for the Friday afternoon concerts; he'd had a messenger

stand in line the day the tickets went on sale, from six o'clock in the morning, and he had gone to town early to take the messenger's place at eight. He had been the first at the window, and there were just two vacant seats for the season. So we had them. We also had a new etching, I said, and Grandmother and Grandfather Kimbrough had given us a new Oriental rug. Mother said that in case of fire, Father and Brother were to roll up the rug and throw it out the window, I was to grab the etching and throw it down on top of the rug, and she would bring the symphony tickets, because they were the most precious of all. I was going to say, too, that we had never lived in an apartment before Chicago; the third floor seemed very high and Mother thought we all ought to be drilled for fire. The girls didn't let me say this. They screamed with laughter and called back and forth across the room, things like, "Wouldn't you just love to see them?" and, "In a fire. A bunch of tickets in your hand. Can't you picture it?"

I wanted to hit them. That's what I got, I thought, for talking so much. But I'd just been answering a question. And we were excited about the symphony tickets. We'd never had anything like that before. Mother and Father had come up to Chicago once for the opera, but the most they could stay was a week, and they certainly hadn't taken me. Now I was going every Friday to a symphony concert, and we had a new etching in our living room, a new Oriental rug that was handsome and stylish. What was so funny about that?

Miss Anne Shaw had a hard time bringing the class to order again, and that made her cross at me. She told me that she hadn't asked me to make a speech. Her questions had been to the class—how many were going to the concerts this year? Raising my hand would have been enough. And if I wanted to speak again, would I please raise my hand for permission?

This was the explanation, then, of the raising-the-hand business I'd noticed in the other classes. At Miss Richey's nobody had raised a hand, probably because there weren't even two of us reciting at the same time. But it was surprising to learn that you not only had to ask permission to leave the room; you even had to ask permission to ask. This was probably what a jail was like, I thought.

I didn't raise my hand because I didn't want to speak again. I would be the one person in the whole Faulkner School, I decided, while Miss Anne Shaw was talking about violins and violas, who would graduate without ever putting up her hand. After that decision I felt better because I was going to be superior to everyone there, and I listened with interest to special phonograph records that had been made to illustrate the sound of each instrument. The class was asked to name the instruments heard, but I didn't put up my hand. When Miss Anne Shaw wanted to know if anyone could identify a passage of music used for one illustration, I could have told them it was the opening of Beethoven's Fifth Symphony and that I knew it because when I'd started to kindergarten, Mother had sung it with the words, "Put on your hat, put on your coat," and had told me what the tune came from. I could have said what some of the other tunes were from, too, but I wasn't going to let them know Mother had been playing them on the piano so that I would recognize them when the time came that we'd be sitting in Orchestra Hall in our own seats at a symphony concert.

We heard the noise of someone coming up the stairs as Miss Anne Shaw was changing a record. She said she would save the record for next time because she heard Mr. Oberndorfer coming to give us Ear Training. She was in such a hurry that she didn't even put away the records, but she met Mr. Oberndorfer part way down the stairs. We heard them say hello and then whisper. Several of the girls nodded their heads in the way that goes with saying, "I know something," and pointed to their ring finger. It wasn't hard to guess that they were signifying to each other that Miss Anne Shaw and Mr. Oberndorfer were in love, but I didn't care if they were or weren't.

The stairs were so steep to the third floor that we saw, from where we sat, Mr. Oberndorfer's face first. It was pink because he was blushing, and he seemed a little out of breath. When the rest of him emerged, I saw that he was small and narrow compared to Miss Anne Shaw. The first thing he told us was to go stand at the far end of the room with our backs to the piano. He said he was going to strike a note, and each girl was to come over in turn and try to strike that note, judging by ear where it would be on the piano. I couldn't believe *my* ears. I had played that game with Mother since I was six, and Brother, who was much better now than I, had been able to do it at three. I could do a simple melody after hearing it once, but Brother could repeat a long, complicated one and could catch the key of a piece on the phonograph without more than two tries. And I was being asked to find one note. I certainly wasn't going to put up my hand for it, however. When Mr. Oberndorfer pointed to me and asked me to try, I decided to go one better than not putting up my hand. I'd hit a note as far off what I heard as I could. I did that, and Mr. Oberndorfer shook his head. He asked if I could carry a tune, and one of the girls said, "She's new, Mr. Oberndorfer. She comes from Muncie, Indiana."

Mr. Oberndorfer nodded his head and went on to the

"She's new, Mr. Oberndorfer. She comes from Muncie, Indiana."

next girl. I decided that they thought we not only didn't have pianos in Muncie, Indiana, we didn't even have ears. I was evidently right, too, because when he found that Katherine Valentine, who was sitting two away from me, couldn't sing a scale, he moved her next to me and skipped us both. At the end of the class he kept me behind to tell me not to be too discouraged; it all might seem very strange and difficult at first, but I would soon get the hang of it. He would help me and before I knew it, I would be able to hear a scale in my head and maybe to sing it. He was so nice I felt somewhat ashamed and almost told him I could do those silly things and had only pretended because I wasn't going to put up a hand again or answer anything so long as I was in the school. If I told about my resolution, however, it would be spoiled, so I only said "thank you" and ran downstairs.

Virginia was waiting on the second floor to take me to French class. She said not to bother about anything Mr. Oberndorfer had said because nobody paid any attention in that class anyway; they just fooled around. I was sorry to hear that because it was the only class that had interested me and that I'd understood. But I told her it certainly wasn't worth bothering about, and we went into a little room where Mademoiselle de la Segliere and the girls were waiting.

Mademoiselle de la Segliere was very thin except for her front. That was enormous. She wore a very tight shirtwaist over it and a watch with a blue enamel fleur-de-lis clasp pinned on it. Her waist was tiny, or perhaps it seemed tinier than it really was, I thought, because her front, just above it, was so big. I noticed all these things while she was calling the roll, and that she wore her hair in a high pompadour, but I didn't hear her mention me until she said loud, "Emily Keeembrrro, I was saying your name."

"Here," I told her quickly, and almost put up my hand, but I remembered in time that I was never going to do that again. Roll-calling was new to me. Miss Richey had never said our names aloud and asked us to tell her that we were present. She could see that we were. But Miss Osgood had said, "I will call the roll. Please raise your hand when your name is called and say 'here' or 'present.' This is for the benefit of the new girls. The rest of you know our custom."

There hadn't been much benefit from it so far as I could see, but at least I knew what calling the roll meant. I wasn't enough accustomed to it, however, to expect it, so I was thinking about something else when my name came. It irritated a teacher to have to say my name several times. Mademoiselle was irritated, I could see, but I wasn't concerned because I knew she wouldn't be troubled by me very long. After this I would remember to listen for my name, and then I would sit without speaking or raising my hand. That certainly couldn't be a bother to anybody.

She asked in French about summer vacations. Had we been to the mountains, to the sea, to the lakes? Clara Cary said she had been to her farm in Wisconsin. Mademoiselle said, "*Bon*," and that we would take for our first vocabulary list the things on a farm. She would say the English word, and we would tell her quickly the French, and after, we would tell her the correct article for each, writing it down in our notebook, masculine or feminine. She pointed a narrow, bony finger at a girl in the back row.

"Horse? *Cheval*. Farm? *Ferme*. Sheep? *Mouton*."

Her finger darted like a dragonfly over the class, quivering in the air for a second and then driving at the girl selected. The finger moved faster and faster, Mademoiselle snapping out the words, the girls breathing short and audibly in excitement, and not another sound in the room. Mademoiselle's finger vibrated in the air and dove at me.

"Cow?" she said, staccato, and clipped to a *k sound*.

"Gosh," I told her.

I hadn't meant to speak at all because of my resolution, but she surprised and scared the word out of me.

The effect of my speaking surprised me more than Mademoiselle's getting it out of me. One or two girls let out their breath in a surprised whistle; some girls squealed with laughter. They all looked uneasily at Mademoiselle. Mademoiselle looked at me, and her face turned bright red. She folded her arms across her large front, pursed up her lips that were thin anyway, and narrowed her eyes at me. When she spoke, she cut off every word, like slicing bread.

"I do not permit," she said, "that anyone in my class shall use a word of slang. You are a new girl here. You will learn that, please. And you will remember also that our girls in this school do not use that word. It is vulgar, *never* for a young lady to say. If you do not know my question, say '*Je ne sais pas.*' That is enough. Another time you use that ugly word, you leave my class. You may all open your notebooks for dictation."

I opened my notebook and put my face as close to it as I could. I hadn't meant to speak, I said over and over to myself, not paying heed to the words Mademoiselle was dictating, and I wouldn't have said any word if Mademoiselle hadn't startled that one out of me. But there wasn't any use trying to explain. Nobody here was on your side. They just waited to pounce on you because you were new and from Muncie, Indiana, instead of Chicago.

The bell rang, and Mademoiselle dismissed the class. I thought I would stay in my seat a second and try to explain, but I decided it was no use. I'd probably just say something else she'd pounce on me for. I got up and left the room, and only said "*au revoir*" as I passed her, the way the other girls had said it as they left.

Virginia was waiting outside for me.

"Don't mind her," she said. "She's really nice, but she gets excited, and she hates slang. I don't think 'Gosh' is so terrible. I've said it myself when Mother couldn't hear me."

"I thought I was saying the word for cow," I told her. "What is it?"

"Oh!" Virginia said, "It's '*vache.*' "

11. Open Sesame

BEGINNING LATIN AT TWELVE-TWENTY WAS THE LAST CLASS. Miss Elizabeth Faulkner taught it. On the first day, when we came into her room on the second floor, I was tired from all the goings on of the morning: upstairs, downstairs, all the strange people, trouble about going for a walk, and teachers, talking, talking, all sounding alike; a different teacher for every subject, but every subject, except Music and Ear Training, sounding like the last. That was the one thing about this school that was like Miss Richey's. No matter how many teachers there were at Miss Faulkner's to say them, the things they said all sounded the same.

Miss Faulkner told us to move our chairs close in around three sides of her desk; the fourth side was against the blackboard. She said that Latin was a language that people talked as well as read and that we were going to do both, so we would sit in a way that made talking easy. First, however, in order to make Latin talking easy we had to learn some verbs and nouns and endings, and she said there was a rhyme about verb endings. Wherever you saw them, you would know that they stood for I, thou, he, we, you, they. It was a key rhyme. Even if you didn't know the meaning of the verb, you would know that I was talking or thou, he, we, you, or they. She recited,

> *M,* or *o, s, t*
> *Mus, tis,* and *n, t.*

For some reason, I felt a sudden shiver in my spine. I must have stared at Miss Faulkner because she stopped talking and wanted to know if I had a question to ask. When I said I didn't want anything except to hear more, she paused again, looked at me, but she only said, "Very well. Here is another rhyme. You're not ready for it yet, but as you come to each of these words, you may remember where it belongs in the rhyme, and so you will know which of these things it means. It's another key.

> Malo, I would rather be
> Malo, in an apple tree,
> Malo, than a wicked man
> Malo, in adversity.

She couldn't have known what was happening to me at that moment. Nobody in the room could know, or in the world, I thought. But it was something like Ali Baba saying "Open Sesame" or the witch saying "Abaca Dabra." "Malo, Malo, Malo" didn't mean anything at all, and yet there was a door opening for me and I was going to walk through it. I could feel it. "M, or o, s, t." It was gibberish, like the counting out,

> Eeny meeny miny mo
> Cracka feeny finey fo
> Oppa, doogia, poppa doogia
> Ick bin ban do
> One, two three,
> And out goes she.

And you were out. Only I was going into something. *M* or *o* were keys. When you found out about them, you found out about a lot of things—by yourself. Nobody said two times two equals four and made you repeat, over and over, all the multiplication tables. For what reason? Everything was always being told you in order for you to say it back. Arithmetic, History, they were all jumbled. One was exactly like the other—hazy, mumbly words. But right now, at this very minute, they were clearing up because of *m* or *o, s, t.*

Miss Faulkner pushed a book into my hand, open at page three. I was so excited that the letters were misty, but when they cleared, I saw, in print, those very letters, *m,* or *o,* next line, *s,* next line, *t.* If you put one on the end of *ama,* you got *amo, amas, amat,* and you were saying, "I love, thou lovest, he loves." If you put two plus two, you got four. If you went west from New York, you got to California. If the Pilgrims arrived in 1620, that meant that in 1620 people called Pilgrims arrived.

"Well," I said aloud, "forevermore." That is a word we said in Muncie when we were surprised.

"Please don't answer that way, Emily, when I ask you a question."

I didn't know she was asking me a question. I'd been too busy. I didn't say anything.

"I have asked you," she repeated, "to turn to page four and read the first sentence in Latin, dividing the words into syllables."

I was only too delighted. The more I could do of this abaca dabra, the more clouds were going to lift. As I turned the page, I said happily, "I don't know what a syllable is."

What I wanted to say was, "I don't know what anything is, but I will. I've got the key—*m* or *o, s, t.* Geography, His-

"Emily, you are evidently trying to make the class laugh."

tory, they're *different* things, and so is Arithmetic, and I'm going to find out about them, and syllables, and bring on any words you can think of."

I didn't say any of those things out loud, but some girls snickered.

"Evidently you're trying to make the class laugh," Miss Faulkner told me, "since of course you know what a syllable is. I understand that this happened in your French class, too. I think you may come back to study hall this afternoon and we will talk about being serious in our work, and we will see what you know about syllables. Virginia, will you read the sentence, please?"

When the bell rang at one o'clock, school was over. The girls were in a rush to go, but they had to wait until Miss Faulkner left the room. As soon as she was gone, they crowded to the door, but several snickered on the way past me. One girl stopped and said I really was a sketch. Where did I come from? I said Muncie, and she asked where that was. I told her Indiana, and she said,

"Oh, a Hoosier hayseed. No wonder. 'Forevermore.' "

She screamed the word at a girl ahead of her, and several others took it up. They all pushed past me except Virginia. She said I had better stay for lunch since I had to see Miss Faulkner, and she would fix it with Miss Daley. She explained that you were supposed to give her your name the first thing in the morning if you wanted to stay for lunch, but that I couldn't have known Miss Faulkner was going to jump on me.

On the way downstairs she told me that she felt awful about the whole thing. If they hadn't all laughed, Miss Faulkner wouldn't have got mad, but, she said, I *had* been funny, saying "forevermore" like that, right out loud, and then telling Miss Faulkner I didn't know what a syllable was.

There was no use trying to convince Virginia that I hadn't meant to be funny because I would have had to explain what had happened, and I couldn't. Besides, I was saying under my breath, "*m* or *o, s, t,*" and it was working. Something Miss Osgood had said in History was coming back to me and making sense, and Miss Farr in Geography, and Arithmetic. Each had its own *m* or *o,* so of course they were different.

Miss Daley was the school secretary. Her office was a desk at the foot of the stairs. Virginia took me to it and talked to her about my staying for lunch. After Virginia left, I stopped thinking *m* or *o* for a minute and remembered that I ought to telephone Mother to tell her, too, because she would be expecting me to be out of school at one o'clock. I asked Miss Daley where the telephone was. She directed me to a corner under the stairs and handed me a nickel. I thought it was nice of her to give me a nickel just because I was a new girl, and I told her so. She looked surprised, and some girls standing around her desk started to laugh. One of them said, "That's the Hoosier hayseed. I guess they don't have telephones where she comes from."

Another one said, "Probably they're so used to hog calling, they just stick their heads out of doors and call when they want to telephone."

Everybody shrieked at that.

Miss Daley told me that I had to put the nickel in a slot in order to telephone. We certainly did not have that kind of telephone in Muncie. I couldn't find the slot, and I had to come back to Miss Daley to ask her to help me. Miss Daley was annoyed, but she showed me.

Mother was angry. She wasn't very proud of me, she said,

first, to have given everyone such a scare by walking out of school, and as if that weren't enough, to have been so naughty that I had to be kept after school the very first day. Since nobody had ever been kept after school at Miss Richey's because she took us to school and brought us home, it hadn't occurred to me that there was any disgrace about it until Virginia had said she felt awful about it, and now Mother. I was surprised. I had thought only that it would be fun to stay at school and eat lunch. I had never done that. Most of all, though, I was excited about going back to Miss Faulkner for some more *m* or *o, s, t.* I was going to try to explain to her how different everything was going to be, separated and clear and right there where you could find out about it, like opening a door in a railroad station marked "waiting room," and there was the waiting room. I didn't tell Mother that on the telephone, but I did say that I had just found out something exciting—I would describe it to her when I got home—and that there was nothing disappointing about staying for study hall. Miss Faulkner only wanted to talk some more about the things I was going to tell Mother when I got home. It was part of the exciting news.

Mother said, was I sure? I repeated that of course I was sure.

Since Virginia didn't stay for lunch, I didn't know anybody. I didn't know either that you had to run to get into the dining room before it was filled, so I had to wait for second sitting and ate with some kindergarteners who stayed for lunch and nap. I got into a little trouble, too, because when an older girl came out of the dining room and asked what I was hanging around for, I said I was waiting for dinner. She called to three friends of hers coming out of the dining room. Then she asked me the same question again, and I answered the same.

"She says 'dinner,' " she repeated to them. They screamed with laughter.

"You'll have a pretty long wait," one of them said, and another one asked me, "Are you sure the Faulkners have invited you?"

I remembered then that in Chicago you had to say lunch and dinner, not dinner and supper. I mumbled that I meant lunch, and they let me go on in. I heard one of the girls ask who I was and another one say, "That's our new little Hoosier hayseed."

I thought if they died shrieking in agony, I would be happy.

Miss Faulkner wasn't ready for me until about an hour after lunch so I wandered about the house. There wasn't any study hall the first day; I think she had forgotten that when she told me to report to her in the afternoon. Only the teachers and some of the seniors and juniors had stayed, except for the special kindergarteners. The juniors and seniors were organizing class activities, Miss Daley said, but I couldn't talk long to her because she was busy. I walked around, but I didn't dare go off the school grounds again so I just wandered until Miss Faulkner remembered and sent for me.

She was kind. She told me first of all that she hoped very much that I would like being at Faulkner, that I would make lots of friends and learn quickly the customs of the school. That was why she had thought it was important for us to talk the very first day so that I would understand that in class we didn't try to distract attention by making people laugh and that we paid attention ourselves. So I mustn't, when she was talking, say things like "forevermore." That wasn't a very suitable expression anyway for a little girl like me—and I mustn't pretend not to know words like syllable. That was not funny; it was rude. Now would I tell her what a syllable was?

I said I didn't know what a syllable was.

She frowned and tightened her lips.

I didn't want her to be cross. I wanted her to know the exciting thing that had happened to me in her own class. I wanted to tell her all kinds of things, how different everything was in Chicago, but that I didn't care now because of *m* or *o, s, t*. It was a charm, it was opening doors, you could do everything with it. School was going to be wonderful because of it. School was for learning things. Learning was exciting. *You* learned; teachers didn't tell you. I wanted to tell her all those things, but I didn't know how. I said, "I get mixed up with words *for* things—syllable, participle, multiple. They were all alike until this morning. I like words *about* things. Mother always says 'not the first.' That means, 'Don't use the first word you think of. Look a little farther back in your mind for another word that will say more exactly what you wanted the first to say.' So I like words like horrifying, meticulous, abominable. But when they mean *things,* I get mixed up. I thought all the things they meant were the same, too, until this morning, and jumbled. But I don't now, because *m* or *o, s, t,* is Latin, and Arithmetic is Arithmetic, and History is different."

Miss Faulkner interrupted me.

"I'm trying to understand," she said. "I know you want to tell me something. But do you know what *m* or *o, s, t,* are? That they're verb endings?"

"Oh, yes, Miss Faulkner," I told her impatiently. "I know that because of Greek."

"Do you know Greek?" Miss Faulkner asked.

I explained about that—how Mother had taught me to read Greek before I had learned to read English because she said that I was bound to learn English and that all letters looked peculiar to children when they were learning to make them. Therefore Greek letters would look no more peculiar than English. So she had taught me the Greek alphabet first, and then to read, and finally to translate, so I had had to learn about verb endings. They were how you found out how to go about opening the secret.

"The secret?" Miss Faulkner didn't seem to understand.

"*Yes,*" I said vehemently. "That's what I found out this morning. Greek is a secret until you know the *m* or *o, s, t,* of it. Latin's like it, with a secret. Everything is different. Everything has one. Two times two for Arithmetic. Everything isn't all jumbled up; it's separate. You just have to find out, that's all. And you can do it by yourself."

Unexpectedly Miss Faulkner kissed me.

"Don't take it too hard," she said. "You've climbed a mountain today. You're out of breath. The view from where you stand is too big to take in all at once. Run home now. And don't say 'forevermore'."

I ran almost all the way home. I didn't care that nobody who passed me knew that my name was Emily Kimbrough and that I came from Muncie, Indiana. I didn't care about dinner instead of lunch, and I had a friend. Virginia was her name.

"*M* or *o, s, t,*" I sang aloud all the three flights up to our apartment and rushed through the door when Hilda opened it.

"Where's Mother?" I demanded. "I've got a surprise to tell her. It's important."

12. *My Friend*

THE FIRST WEEK OF SCHOOL DID NOT PRODUCE FRIENDS the way I had expected. Virginia Cornwall talked to me and I had a few conversations with a girl who had bright pink cheeks and yellow braids that she could sit on. I pointed her out one day when Mother came to call for me, and Mother said she looked exactly like a Gari Melchers. I told Mother that her name was Ruth Huey and that she was the best athlete in the whole school and that she had said she might try to teach me how to play guard in basketball. I was not good in athletics, even at dumb-bell exercises. Another girl, who sometimes walked with me from one class to another, was named Clara Cary. She was very tall and had soft, curly hair. I thought she was stunning. She told me that she liked horses more than any other animals, or people, and that she had three beauties of her own on her father's farm in Wisconsin. Her father was a doctor, she said, and couldn't go to the farm very often, but she went every vacation and all summer. One day she said she might ask me sometime to visit her at the farm. I resolved to make some mention of this every day so that the idea would not slip her mind. Marguerite Fellows was another girl in my class who spoke to me the first week, but she had so many

friends in every class that she didn't have much time for
me. She was always rushing from one friend to another to
get the news.

The first girl to ask me over to her house to play was
Katharine Valentine, but when she telephoned me she said,
"This is Katharine." I thought it was Catherine Bannister,
a chum from Muncie, and I screamed at her over the telephone that I was thrilled to hear her voice. She asked,
"Why, for goodness sake? I only wanted to ask you to come
over to my house this afternoon to play basketball."

I was too embarrassed to say I'd thought it was someone
else, and besides I thought that would sound rude. So I
only told her I'd love to come. When I got there, the other
girls she'd asked called out, "Are you thrilled to hear my
voice?" and "What'll you do when *I* telephone you?"

Things like that all afternoon, so I didn't have a very
good time after all. But the next day at recess I told someone in my class who hadn't been there that I'd had a wonderful visit at Katharine Valentine's. I wanted her to think I
had.

"Visit?" she asked. "Did you spend the night?"

"Why, no," I told her. "I went over to play basketball."

She called some other girls to come hear what I'd said.
"Emily goes on a visit," she told them, and repeated it.
They shrieked with laughter, and one of them warned the
others not to ask me over to play because since I went
"visiting," I'd probably bring a suitcase and stay a week.

Just as I'd think I was learning what things not to say
when you lived in Chicago, I'd make another mistake—
like "get to go." In Muncie we said we hoped we'd "get to
go" somewhere or "get to do" something when we were
longing for it, and the sharpest disappointment was when
we "didn't get to go." The girls at Miss Faulkner's thought

this the funniest expression they'd ever heard and repeated it to one another in front of me until I was so sick of it I never wanted to hear, much less say, it again.

Marguerite, Virginia, and Clara were not like that, but I didn't see them much. The third or fourth day of school Ruth Huey asked where I lived, and when I told her, she said it was not far from the Chicago Beach Hotel, where she lived, and asked if I'd like her to drop me off at my house. I was pleased, but when we got there, I couldn't open the door of her car. I banged on it, pretending it was stuck, but she burst out laughing and asked if I didn't know how to open a car. Did we just have horses and buggies in Muncie? That made me mad, and I was hot with embarrassment. I was going to tell her that my grandfather had an automobile. It wasn't a big limousine like hers, but it was a Pierce Arrow. Grandfather didn't have a stylish chauffeur in a uniform like her chauffeur's. Hubert, the hired man, drove, usually wearing a pair of overalls and, winter and summer, a straw hat; but he always got down and opened the door. Grandmother never touched it, and she never let me because, she said, the pesky catch on it could pinch your fingers. Ruth's chauffeur didn't budge from his seat, but Ruth leaned forward and opened the door for me. I didn't tell her about Hubert; I didn't even say thank you. I just jumped out of the car and ran up the steps. In bed that night I decided that she would never ask me again.

She did ask me though. A few days later when she heard some girls ask had I done any visiting lately, she invited me, suddenly, in front of them, to visit her the following Friday, spend the night, and bring my suitcase. Her mother would telephone mine. The girls who had been teasing me were awed because Ruth was the best athlete in the school; even upstairs in the Academic department everybody knew her—seniors spoke to her. I was giddy with pleasure and so exhilarated by this sudden prominence that I swept through an Arithmetic paper and got 100 on it. I stood by Miss Farr's desk while she marked it, a *C* for correct, after the first, second, third problems; by the time she reached the eighth, I was breathing so hard I felt as if I had run to Forty-seventh Street and back; ninth, tenth, eleventh. I had to lean against her because my knees were trembling—seventeenth, eighteenth, nineteenth—my forehead and hands were soaked with sweat, and on the twentieth even her hand shook a little, but she made the biggest *C* of all.

"A perfect paper, Emily," she said. "I'm proud of you. I think you're beginning to understand. You see, you did this carefully. You thought."

I hadn't done it carefully, and I hadn't thought about the Arithmetic. All I could think of was that Ruth Huey had invited me to visit her for the night, RUTH HUEY, and the first time I had ever been asked to spend the night at any girl's house—like having Baked Alaska the first time you ever tasted ice cream. That's what I'd been thinking about. So I hadn't been buffaloed by the problems and followed my usual method of erasing, trying again, rubbing out, and smearing up my whole paper. I didn't explain this to Miss Farr. I just asked her if I could telephone the news to my father. She said I could and that I needn't even wait for recess.

I rushed from the room to Miss Daley's desk at the foot of the stairs. I showed her the paper and explained that Miss Farr had said I could telephone Father. She said the paper was wonderful and showed it to Miss Faulkner who came downstairs at that moment to speak to Miss Daley. Miss Faulkner was pleased. Miss Daley gave me a nickel for the telephone and turned on the light for me so that I could see to read the problems to Father. After he had guaranteed it was a good thing he hadn't been given those problems because he couldn't possibly have done one of them, let alone twenty, I burst in with the news about Ruth's inviting me for the night. I tried to show him how that had been why I'd got the 100, but he didn't seem to understand so I skipped it and asked if he and Mother would let me go. As soon as I said that, I wished with all my might that he hadn't heard me because if he said no, I would die, or run away from school and Chicago, and never come back. The prospect was so terrifying, the biggest thing in my life swept away by his saying no and my whole life changed because of it, that I began to sweat and felt a sort of humming in my ears so that I couldn't hear what he was saying. I wanted to ask him to repeat it, and yet I didn't want him to.

Father said very loud, I heard him through my stopped-up ears, "What's the matter? Are we still connected? I said I thought it would be lovely for you to go to your friend's if Mother says it's all right. I know her father."

I said thank you in a hoarse voice that didn't sound in the least like mine. I hung up the telephone and stood in front of it for a minute or two because I was too dazed to move.

My father knew her father. I hadn't supposed that any father in Chicago knew anyone else's father, with the children knowing each other. I'd thought it was only that way in Muncie, families knowing families. I'd never heard anyone at Miss Faulkner's say anything like, "My mother wants you to tell your mother—"

Things like that to show that the mothers knew each other—especially when there were so many children as there were at Miss Faulkner's and, consequently, so many parents. I'd thought that children finally got to know one another, and parents knew other people. And then, of all things, to have my own father know another father, especially to know the father of the best athlete at Miss Faulkner's and the one girl who had asked ME to spend my first night at any girl's house. It just went to show, I thought, still standing in front of the telephone, that you really knew nothing about your parents at all. Father had a friend in Chicago. His name was Mr. Huey. His daughter was going to take me to their house. Why, at this rate someone might stop me on the street one day and ask if I were Hal Kimbrough's daughter, and it would be a friend of father's.

Two or three girls came running around the corner to use the telephone, and I realized it was recess period. There was always a long line of girls in front of the telephone at recess, calling home to ask if they could go to a friend's house from school or stay to lunch or be stopped for at a different time. Except for the first day when I had let Mother know that I was being kept after school, I'd had no reason to use the telephone. This was an important day.

I moved away to let the first girl make her call and said to her casually, "I was just telephoning to ask about going to Ruth Huey's house for—" and I didn't say "visit." I said, "For the night. And I—" I remembered not to say, "I got to go." I said, "—and I'm going."

"I wish I were you."

Those were her words. To ME! All in all it was a beautiful day.

Friday was just as good because all morning people said things like, "You're going to spend the night at Ruth's, aren't you?"

And I answered, "Uh-huh. Her mother talked to mine."

I didn't think they cared that her mother had talked to mine, but I liked to say it. Saying it made the Kimbrough family sound established in Chicago, like other people. The telephone ringing, someone asking for my mother, Mother saying "hello," and it wasn't the grocer or the cleaner but Mrs. Huey, talking about her daughter and me.

When Ruth and I left school on Friday, several girls waved good-by to us. I felt like a picture of Queen Mary I had seen in the *Ladies' Home Journal*. She was in her car, waving to the people watching her. So I waved the way she did in the picture, with the palm of my hand turned in and the fingers bent, and I leaned forward to make this gesture out the side window. That was what Queen Mary had done.

We stopped at the apartment to pick up my suitcase. I said good-by to Mother and Hilda. Mother said she would telephone me in the morning, but Hilda said anyone would think I was going off for a week.

The Chicago Beach Hotel was bigger than the Del Prado and much grander. Ruth's family had a whole apartment in it, living room, library, dining room, and bedrooms. You could see the lake from every one of them.

"Sumptuous," I said to myself.

Mrs. Huey looked like Ruth except that her hair was dark instead of blonde. She said she was so glad I could come and glad that Ruth and I were friends. I wanted to throw my arms around her because this was the first time it had been said aloud that I had a friend. I didn't. I said thank you and that Mother had sent her love. Mother hadn't, but I wanted to give a boost to this friendship.

Mrs. Huey was wearing a beautiful long pale blue dress with lace around the collar and cuffs. I knew from pictures that this was a tea gown, but I had never seen one before.

We agreed that he was exactly our type.

She sat in a big chair by the window and had a pile of books on a small table beside her. Ruth called her "Dearie." When we left her and went into Ruth's room, Ruth said her mother was sort of an invalid. I had never seen an invalid before nor heard a mother called anything but Mother.

"Very impressive," I said to myself.

We changed our clothes to middy blouse, bloomers, and gym shoes. Ruth said we could fool around on the beach if I wanted to. We walked out of the hotel through a passageway and were immediately at the lake. In front of us there was a row of little shanties, or that's what we would have called them in Indiana, but Ruth said they were lockers. They were close to the hotel with a boardwalk between, and on the other side of them were the sand and the water. Ruth opened the door of one of the shanties with a key she wore on a string around her neck and brought out a basketball. She said this would be a good time and place for me to practice guarding and catching.

A man came up while we were practicing and asked if he could play basketball with us. We'd noticed him when we came out because he was doing gymnastics and all sorts of stunts, like handstands and back flips, somersaults in the air, and long jumps. He was dressed all in white, sweater, flannel trousers, and shoes. His skin was very tanned, his hair black, and Ruth had said he had the most magnificent build she had ever seen. I'd said I had never seen such a handsome man. We'd agreed that he was exactly our type. Then we had started to practice and hadn't noticed him again. When he came over to us we were surprised. I said to Ruth afterward that I had thought I was going to swoon. She admitted that she had very nearly swooned, too. We were getting to be better friends every minute.

The man and Ruth were wonderful at throwing and

guarding. They took turns doing it. I was the catcher, but I seldom caught. Each of them threw so hard that I had to go a long way down the beach to retrieve the ball. Once when I came back from one of these hikes, they were sitting down resting while they waited for me. As I was handing him the ball, Ruth said, "Isn't your college open yet?"

The man laughed, and I thought I had never seen such white teeth.

"I don't go to college," he answered. "I'm an actor. My name's Douglas Fairbanks."

The ball rolled out of my hands, but I didn't go after it. Mr. Fairbanks laughed.

"What's the matter?" he asked me. "Haven't you ever talked to an actor before?"

"No," I told him. "But I talked to an actress once— Little Eva, at the Wyser Grand. She sold photographs of herself in the intermission. Ten cents. I bought one, and she spoke to me."

Ruth said quickly, "Why, I know. You're acting in *Officer 666.*"

"That's right." He smiled at both of us. "Would you youngsters like to come to the matinee tomorrow?"

I was able to nod. I couldn't have spoken.

Ruth spoke, though, in a rush. She said we'd love to, but she would have to ask her mother. She was sure her mother would let us, but someone would have to go with us. We wouldn't be allowed to go alone.

"Do you think three tickets would be too much?" she added. "I'm afraid that's very rude."

He said it wasn't at all and that three tickets were not in the least too much. If she would tell her name, he'd be delighted to speak to her mother.

We took him back to the hotel with us that instant. He

came all the way up to the Huey's apartment and spoke to Mrs. Huey. And she said we could go. She was sure Mr. Huey would be delighted to take us. Mr. Fairbanks said there wasn't a thing in the play that wasn't perfectly all right for us to see, he would guarantee it.

When he had gone, Ruth and I repeated to each other every word he had spoken so that we would never forget them. When Mr. Huey came home from his office, we repeated them to him and again to Mrs. Huey. Mr. Huey said he would take us. He also said, "So this is Ruth's friend. I know your father. Glad to see you."

And there was that warm feeling again, running all the way from my head to my stomach. I was a friend, and belonging.

While I was changing to a dress for dinner, Ruth went to speak to her mother. When she came back she told me she had asked if I could stay over the whole week end and not go home until after school on Monday. Mrs. Huey called that she was speaking to Mother on the telephone and that Mother wanted to talk to me. The first thing I said to her was, "Hello, Mother, did you have a nice time talking to Mrs. Huey?"

Mrs. Huey was in the room and laughed. So did Mother. I was trying to tell her that maybe talking twice to the same person on the telephone was making Mother friends with her, so that Mother was having a nice time along with me. Mother asked if I were being polite and considerate and said that I could stay until Monday. The minute I'd hung up the telephone I ran back and told Ruth. Suddenly we hugged each other, and then she gave me a wide patent leather belt of hers to wear and I gave her a plaid hair ribbon.

We had dinner in the Huey's dining room, though I had

hoped we would go downstairs to the big one since I was wearing my new belt. After dinner Mr. and Mrs. Huey took us to see the *Adventures of Kathleen* at the Fifty-first Street moving picture theater. Mrs. Huey walked slowly, Mr. Huey and Ruth on either side of her.

Ruth and I talked a long time in bed, about school and the teachers and moving pictures we liked. But I didn't say anything of how I felt about Muncie and Chicago because I preferred her to think that they were just the same. She went to sleep before me.

Saturday morning Ruth and I had breakfast downstairs in the big dining room at a table looking out on the lake. Ruth said I could order anything I wanted; she always had the same breakfast every day, and her waiter knew what it was—an alligator pear with French dressing, iced tea, and English muffins. It was not a breakfast I would have thought of, but since we were friends, I decided we ought to eat the same things. They made a delicious combination, and I told Ruth I was going to see if we couldn't have them at home.

After breakfast I bought picture post cards of the Chicago Beach Hotel and wrote them in the writing room. I sent one to my Grandmother and Grandfather Kimbrough and my best friend in Muncie, Betty Ball, Grandmother Wiles in Indianapolis, and to Mother, Father, Brother, and our maid, Hilda, at 5019 Blackstone Avenue, Chicago. I thought of walking around to our apartment with the ones for my family and dropping them in our mailbox so that I wouldn't have to buy stamps, but I decided that the pleasure they would have from receiving them by regular mail justified the additional expense.

We went downtown in the car and had lunch with Mr. Huey in the Mother Goose Room at the Tip Top Inn. I was too excited about the theater to be able to eat much, and that was exasperating. I would have preferred to have these events spread out a little. We even had to hurry, and it was my first visit to a restaurant. But Mr. Huey pushed us along. As it was, we were scarcely in our seats before the curtain went up.

Our seats were in a box. Ruth and I leaned as far as we could over the rail in case Mr. Fairbanks wanted to see us. At the end of the first act he bowed exactly at us. We both of us very nearly went all the way over the rail when he did that. From then on I lost the thread of the plot.

Mr. Huey talked about the play on the way home. He thought it one of the funniest comedies he'd seen in a long time. Ruth and I didn't say much; we were both lost in our thoughts and dreams. When we got home I heard Mr. Huey tell Ruth's mother that maybe the play had been a little over our heads; he wasn't sure we'd enjoyed it. He and Mrs. Huey played Flinch with us after dinner. It was one of my favorite games, but I wasn't in the mood for it.

I put myself to sleep by creating a life for Mr. Fairbanks and me, dancing and singing, I dazzling everyone with my grace and beauty when he tossed me in the air as I sang high C in a trill.

Next morning I did not disclose to Ruth this plan for the future, but when I came home from Sunday school, she and I wrote a letter to Douglas, as I called him privately, thanking him for the theater tickets and telling him our estimate of his artistic ability. The letter took a little over two hours to write, but we were pleased with it. Each of us wrote every other line, in ink, of course, though the first twenty drafts had been in pencil.

The rest of the day was dull. We did our homework in the afternoon and after that, walked and walked on the

beach; we weren't allowed to play with the basketball because it was Sunday. Nobody else came on the beach so
when it got dark, we came in. We were tired, and we
decided it was unlikely that anyone would come out to do
exercises or play games after dark.

By noon on Monday I came to the conclusion that, not
counting Saturday, I was in the middle of the most beautiful day in my life. Practically every girl in the Intermediate
department had asked me about my week end with Ruth,
and I hadn't used the word "visit" once. At recess four
seniors had come downstairs to ask if it were true that
Douglas Fairbanks had played basketball with us and invited us to the matinee. Between Music and Latin, the
captain of the basketball team, who was also a senior, had
slipped a note into my hand asking if I could stay for
basketball practice that afternoon and try out for substitute
guard. When I showed it to Ruth she seemed a little
worried. She said she wished there had been more time to
work on me but for me not to try to catch the ball myself,
just jump up and down in front of my forward, if I thought
I could do that. I said I thought I could. I told Miss Daley
about Douglas Fairbanks so she didn't mind my signing
up late to stay for lunch. Mother said on the telephone
that it was all right for me to stay.

The captain of the basketball team asked me to sit at
her table for lunch and after lunch to go to Cunag's on
Forty-seventh Street for a double hot fudge marshmallow
as dessert. I felt a little sick, but I knew it was from
the general excitement and that hot fudge marshmallow
wouldn't make any difference. Ruth said for us to go ahead;
she wanted to telephone Dearie and would catch up with
us. I walked with the captain.

The popcorn man was standing on the corner as we came

out. He came nearly every day, pushing a cart that had glass windows and a flame in the middle. He popped corn over the flame in a wire popper, tied to the ceiling with a string, so he only had to shake the handle; and after it was popped and scooped into a bag, he poured melted butter on it from an agate coffee pot. The butter only went around the top; the rest of the bag was stone dry. He knew this always made me mad so he called out as we came down the steps that if I'd buy a bag, he'd butter it all the way down. I was a good customer; sometimes I'd even shaken the popper because when I'd been standing around before school with no one talking to me, it had given me something to do. But I said no, not today. I was going to Cunag's. He looked so disappointed that I told him all right, I'd buy a bag later, and it occurred to me at that instant that of course I ought to take presents home since I'd been away on a visit. Mother and Father always brought home presents when they'd been away; Grandmother and Grandfather, every winter after they'd been South; people took home presents after a trip. Popcorn would be fine for Brother, and at Cunag's I'd get a box of candy for Mother and Father—they could share it—and an all-day sucker for Hilda.

I asked the popcorn man if he'd wait until I got back from Cunag's, I didn't want to carry it all the way. He said he would. I explained my plan to the captain because I didn't want her to think I was postponing buying the bag so I wouldn't have to share it. She said, when I'd finished explaining, "Excuse me a minute. I'll just tell the other girls so they'll understand."

The other girls were walking behind us. She ran back to them but joined me again when we reached Cunag's, and said they understood perfectly.

They all seemed to have a regular table, but I had never been there before. Mr. Cunag was a Greek and very hospitable. He called most of the girls by name. When my turn came, I ordered a double hot fudge marshmallow like everyone else, only without nuts, because with the way the day was going, I didn't entirely trust my stomach. After Mr. Cunag had finished writing down what we wanted, I said to everybody that I guessed I'd order the box of candy I was buying for Mother and Father. I said it that way so that they would know why I couldn't open it and give everyone a piece.

I went over to the candy counter. The lady there said she was Mrs. Cunag and what could she do for me? I'd never bought a box of candy, but a bag didn't seem proper for a present. I picked out first the all-day sucker for Hilda while I was making up my mind about how to choose the candy, and then I said I would like that box—I indicated the one I wanted—filled with—and I began my selection from the trays in the case.

"Two cents' worth of those, a penny's worth of those, maybe three cents' of those."

A scream of laughter from the table I'd left made me lose count and whirl around to what was going on and share the fun. Simultaneously, Ruth came in the door. The girls were doubled up, rocking back and forth, and only the captain seemed able to speak. She squealed, "Honestly, Ruth, she'll be the death of us. Two cents' of this, a penny's worth. She's buying a *box* of candy that way."

Another girl broke in, louder than the captain, "Do you know *why*? *Presents* for her family, because she's spent the week end with you."

Someone else screamed about the popcorn.

Ruth came over to me.

"When you buy candy by the pound," she said, "you just pick out the kinds you want and ask to have the box filled with them. Aren't you ever going to get over being a rube?"

The girl filled the box and I waited at the counter for it. Ruth went on to the table. I called over to her and the others that Mother had told me I couldn't stay for basketball. I was terribly sorry, and I hadn't realized how late it was so I couldn't even stay to eat my sundae. I told her to pay for it, and I'd pay her back; I was in a hurry. I didn't take the candy. I walked to the door. As I reached it, Ruth got up from the table, and came toward me, but as soon as I'd opened the door, I commenced to run. She couldn't have caught up with me, I had such a head start. I ran all the way back to school and was going past it when the popcorn man called me. He had the bag ready so I took it. But I didn't go into school for my books. I ran almost all the rest of the way home, and when I got there, I threw up. Mother made me go straight to bed. I said I'd come home because I felt sick and hadn't stopped for my books because I was afraid I was going to throw up. Mother said that was all right; she'd go back for them. She said they had enjoyed the post cards.

When Father got home from the office, he came in with Mother to see me. I told them I didn't want any supper.

"She simply can't stand excitement," Mother said.

13. A Rustic and a Fairy

WHEN I CAME INTO THE BUILDING ON THE THIRD MONDAY after the opening of school, Marguerite Fellows was outside the door of our room. She told me she had been waiting for me, and I was gratified.

"I've got news for you," she said. "Your desk mate's arrived. And she says she knows you. Her name's Bower Kelly."

Marguerite would have gone on to give me her impression of Bower because she loved describing people, but I didn't wait to listen. I rushed into the room and to my desk. I couldn't believe that my desk mate was actually going to be Bower. But she was there, pasting a schedule on the cover of her notebook. I hadn't seen her since we'd moved to Blackstone Avenue, and I couldn't have been more surprised and delighted if my desk mate had turned out to be someone from Muncie.

She was pleased, too, but not excited, and when I had calmed down a little, she explained that her mother had decided during the summer to transfer her from the Kenwood Institute School for Girls to the Faulkner School, but that two weeks before our term began, she had been taken ill. That was why she was late in starting.

I immediately assumed complete proprietorship over her, and introduced her to the members of my class, as if she and they were equally old friends of mine.

At recess I took her and another new girl, Eleanor Donnelly, to Barby and explained to both of them about the cocoa and the difficulty of getting to it in time for the foam on top. Someone had told me that Eleanor did not live in Chicago, but was staying at her grandmother's, a few blocks away, in order to come to school at Miss Faulkner's. I imagined how she must be feeling, coming to a strange place like Chicago, so to make things easier for her and Bower, who was nearly three weeks behind, I told them a few things about Faulkner customs and peculiarities to look out for.

"I found out about one of them myself," I said, "only a week ago, and in connection with the foam on the cocoa."

I'd been working on an arithmetic problem just before recess, I explained, an occupation that always demanded my intense concentration, though it was usually fruitless. Therefore, I had not seen Miss Faulkner come into the room and go up to the desk to speak to Miss Farr. My attention had only been caught by the sound of desk chairs scraping on the floor. I'd looked up to see all the girls getting to their feet, and had noticed that Miss Faulkner was talking to Miss Farr. What had struck me, however, was that the moment had come to put into action a plan I had had in mind for some time. I had, accordingly, bolted from the room and made for Barby at top speed. I was going to be first in line for the cocoa.

Barby had been surprised to see me; she'd said her watch must be slow, but that the cocoa was ready. She'd put the egg beater in the big caldron and turned it hard. I had had two cups of nothing but foam. It had been as exquisite as I had thought it would be.

Just as I had finished the second cup and was talking to Barby, a senior monitor had come in and told me she had been looking for me, because Miss Faulkner wanted to see me in her office.

I'd put down my cocoa and sidled past her. But once out the door, I'd begun to run up the stairs. At that moment, the recess bell had rung, and I'd realized that I hadn't heard it before. The girls had come swarming down the stairs. I hadn't been able to push past them going the other way, so I'd stood close to the bannister, holding on to keep from being knocked down. Several, when they went past, had asked me if I had got to the fire.

I'd found Miss Faulkner sitting at her desk. She'd told me to come in, but hadn't asked me to sit down. I'd stood beside her desk and she'd looked at me sternly for what had seemed to me a very long time, before she'd asked what reason I could give her for having run out of the room when she had come in. I'd told her it was because I'd thought it was recess.

"Had the bell rung?" she'd asked.

I'd said that I hadn't heard it but that everybody had stood up.

Then she'd asked me if I hadn't seen her come into the room. I'd told her I hadn't, and that no one had said anything to me about her taking us somewhere.

"Taking you somewhere?" she'd repeated.

I'd said, "Yes, Miss Faulkner, when they all stood up to go."

Then she'd explained that they'd all stood up just because she had come into the room. She must have seen how astonished I felt, because she'd asked if I didn't stand up when my mother or any older person came into the room. I'd said no, I didn't, that I'd never heard of such a thing. Miss Faulkner had spoken kindly then. Perhaps it was a sophisticated custom prevailing more in cities than in small communities, but certainly she had thought that well-brought-up children anywhere always rose when an older person came into the room and remained standing until that person had either sat down, left the room, or asked the child to be seated. She'd wanted to know if that was clear to me. I'd said it was. She'd dismissed me with a little pat on my arm, saying she was sure I would not forget this rule.

I was sure that I would not forget it either, but I had been so mad that after leaving her office I'd gone downstairs and out into the schoolyard. Nobody else was there. I'd walked round and round, until I'd heard the end of recess bell, and I had had very satisfactory imaginary conversation with Miss Faulkner, in which I had told her something about well-brought-up children in Muncie. That we wouldn't dare talk back to grown-ups the way some of these well-brought-up girls who stood up talked back to the teacher. And we had to say, "Yes, mother," or "Yes, father," or yes, anybody, not just "yes" or "no" or "uh-uh." We weren't allowed to answer back or break into conversation. When somebody came into the room we gave up the chair we were sitting on, if it was the most comfortable, but we certainly didn't stand up just to be standing up. I'd told her, too, that we didn't bow, either, in case she wanted to know, or sit on our knees the way they did in China or Japan, but as far as I could see it would be a lot easier to live in either of those places than in Chicago. In those places they wouldn't expect you to know every little Chinese or Japanese custom, the way Miss Faulkner expected you to.

I didn't repeat this conversation to Bower and Eleanor, but when I had told them the other part of the incident,

I said, "Now you know the kind of thing that happens all the time in this school and in Chicago. Did you ever hear of anything so silly?"

To my stupefaction, Eleanor said that it didn't seem silly to her. In Lake Forest, where she lived, children always stood up, and even Bower told me that in New Orleans they did, too. She added that she guessed I hadn't noticed it at the Del Prado, because children and grown-ups weren't together very much in a hotel, the way they were in your own house.

They wanted to know what other Faulkner customs there were. I decided to let them find out for themselves, and told them I couldn't think of any at the moment.

On the Wednesday of that week we had our first dancing class. Miss Lee taught it in the gymnasium. While we were waiting in the hall outside for the group that preceded ours to be dismissed, Ruth Huey told me Miss Lee ought to be good because she was one of Miss Hinman's teachers. I had never heard of Miss Hinman and asked who she was. Ruth answered that she supposed everyone knew who Miss Hinman was, because she had several studios in Chicago where she taught teachers and private students in both ballroom and fancy dancing. When you were old enough to join a social dancing class with boys at someone's house, Miss Hinman conducted it.

The class was dismissed while we were talking, and our line began to file in. As we moved along I said over my shoulder to Ruth, who was behind me, that Miss Hinman hadn't conducted a class in Muncie, so why should I have known her?

I faced back again to discover that I had come to the doorway of the gym, and that a woman standing there, who

I supposed was Miss Lee, was extending her hand to me. I shook it and prepared to pass on, but she detained me.

"Where is our curtsy?" she asked.

I could have told her that I hadn't the faintest idea where it was, and furthermore that I didn't know *what* it was, but I only mumbled that I guessed I'd forgotten it.

Her answer was, "Well, we won't forget it next time, will we, whenever we speak to someone older than ourselves?"

I moved down to join the line of girls already in the gymnasium. Several of them snickered, and one of them started a kind of rhyme: "Muncie doesn't curtsy."

Others took it up.

I didn't mind the rhyme much because I was preoccupied, dumbfounded at the things children in Chicago were put to. The rhyme was right; Muncie didn't curtsy. At our ballroom dancing class there we had simply shaken hands with the teacher. Mother had been very fussy about how it was done.

"Look at the person with whom you're shaking hands," she had said again and again, and had made me practice it on her. "*Shake* hands firmly. Don't just put out a limp paw for someone to take, with all the weight of your arm in it."

No one had said anything about a curtsy. I watched for Ruth who had been behind me in line to pass Miss Lee. She curtsied; so did the next, and the next after her. They hadn't forgot their curtsies. I not only didn't have one ready, I'd never seen one. The nearest I had ever come to it in Muncie was when Betty Ball and I had danced a minuet in a school play at Miss Richey's. Had Miss Lee told me to make a curtsy instead of asking where mine was, I would have pulled my gym bloomers out at each side as far as they would go and have sunk to the floor. The lackadaisical dip these girls were making had not the style, I thought, I would have given her. But I was discouraged to realize how easily they did it.

I noticed that some dipped the left knee and some the right, and that Miss Lee didn't care. Evidently there was no rule about this. I wondered how a girl decided which one to dip and at what moment she made the decision. I was, however, too dispirited to care much, because this was just one more thing to catch on to, and there were probably others I hadn't heard about.

That evening I surprised Mother by trying out a curtsy on her. She had come into my room to tell me Hilda had announced supper, and that after we had finished she was going to play the *Ring* music again for Brother and me. I had been standing in front of my bureau, when she stepped in, but I sat down quickly on a chair near it. Then I stood up again to show her what I now did when older people came into the room, but she was talking about the *Ring* music and didn't notice. So I decided, on the spur of the moment, to demonstrate my latest accomplishment. I walked across the room to her, anticipating with a condescending pity, her surprise. I put out my hand, but as I did this I changed my dip from the knee I had originally intended. The resulant confusion threw me off balance, so that I lurched into her, caught her unaware, and sent her backward across my bed.

She was annoyed because she thought I was practicing one of Brother's jujitsu tricks. When I explained what my purpose had been, she was mollified, but she urged me to put in more practice on it before I used it outside the family. She added that she had never taught me to curtsy because she considered it affected and a little absurd. If the other girls did it, however, I might as well. I was surprised to know that she had heard of it.

After supper Brother and I played the game Mother had evolved for the purpose of teaching us the motifs from *The Ring*. The Chicago Opera Company was going to give the entire series later in the winter. Our whole family was going. We already had our tickets, but Mother had decided that Brother and I would derive a greater amount of esthetic benefit and would justify more satisfactorily the expenditure, if we were somewhat familiar with the music beforehand. She'd prefaced the game by playing the principal motifs from the opera over and over with one finger until Brother and I had absorbed them sufficiently to move on to the next step. This had been the allotment to each of us of several parts. Then, according to the game, we were to wait in the hall outside the living room. She would play, but not with just one finger, excerpts from the music. When the motif of a particular character was played, the one to whom that character had been allotted was to rush into the living room and act out something to do with the role. A missed cue, or a failure to put the proper characters to the motif, cost five points. Our scores were totaled at the end of each evening's game.

Brother had the part of the Dragon, the Dwarf, the Sword, the Fire, Siegfried, et cetera. I had Brünnehilde, the Rhine Maidens, the Rhine, the Love Motif and a few lesser ones. The role I favored was the Valkyrie Cry. Brother and I had fought from the beginning over which one came in the more frequently, but on the evening of that first dancing class, he threatened to give up the game because of my performance. Responding to the cue of the Rhine Maidens' motif, I made my entrance in a series of curtsies. Reaching in this fashion the center of the living room, I flowed into the first steps of the buck and wing that Miss Lee had taught us during the afternoon. Brother said that no one had ever seen a Rhine Maiden nor anybody else swim like that, but Mother squelched his voluble protests by ordering that as long as I came in on my cue, he was not to quibble at my interpretation. By the time we were sent to bed, I was dipping with confidence.

The following week I had become proficient enough to curtsy to Miss Lee without unbalancing either of us, though my contact with her looked more like a thrust and parry than a social greeting. I counted this no deterrent to my thorough enjoyment of the dancing class. Our costume was comprised of blue serge bloomers, white middy blouses, black ribbed stockings and ballet slippers laced round our ankles. I would have preferred something in chiffon, but I was not so held down by these accouterments that I could not think of myself as Pavlova.

In the spirit of Pavlova I learned the buck and wing to the tune of "A Bit of A Brogue," and a Spanish dance entitled "The Cachucha." I was even selected out of the whole class to do an Irish dance with Bower, on parents' day. I told Mother that she would see for herself that I performed with more verve than Bower. At the exhibition, however, our finale was marred because I had laced my ballet slippers with green ribbons, crossed all the way up to my knees to give the effect of an Irish costume, and in the last step, that was spirited to the point of violence, the lacings came down, tripped me up because I stepped on them, and tripped Bower because I grabbed her to keep from falling.

There were other exhibitions during the term for which solos were allotted, but I was not selected for these.

The following year, however, I was told that I had progressed sufficiently both in my dancing and dependability, to dance in a school play, provided my marks were up to the level required.

My progress in academic subjects was as uneven as my dancing. I had left Arithmetic by a scant passing and a considerable boosting from Miss Farr, for effort. Miss Osgood then took me on for Algebra. On the day she urged me not to drop my signs and I obediently brought her an answer of plus zero, she told me that she almost despaired of my ever understanding that subject.

Geography also routed me. I had scarcely begun it at Miss Richey's, when we moved from Muncie. But at Miss Faulkner's, it was taught in the sixth grade. I was expected, therefore, to know something of the countries of the world. I not only knew nothing of them, I didn't know how to go about finding them on a map. In the study of Ancient History this put me at a distinct disadvantage. The Island of Delos was a particularly tricky little spot to find, until I clinched its location by ascertaining that it was three blobs down and two across, but from what I hadn't the remotest idea. And no sooner had I marked the location than I was given another map of the same area but on a larger scale, a term in itself that I had never heard. Counting three down and two across I came up in a territory far removed from Delos. If I were given a map, furthermore, in which Egypt was not pink, I could not find Egypt.

But Latin set up for me no such foolish obstacles, and I felt at home there from the day I heard the key rhyme, m or o, s, t. I knew too, on that day, that Miss Faulkner was an exciting teacher, and that this was what made Latin, and Greek as well, unmitigated delight.

Bower and I were the only girls who took Greek, and Miss Faulkner worked us into her schedule by teaching us during a period when she took charge of study hall. We would have been somewhat conspicuous and distracting on the dais where the teacher's desk was, so Miss Faulkner placed us behind a piano that stood in one corner of the room and was used for morning assembly exercises. From there she could keep an eye on the girls studying in the room, and answer the questions of those who came tiptoeing around the piano for help in whatever they were studying. Bower and I were scarcely aware of the interruption. We were having fun in a subject that Miss Faulkner drenched in her own enthusiasm and fervor.

My English teacher told me that I ran off the track in my themes, and wrote about everything but the subject given me. "Vaporizing," she called it. She also urged that when asked for a theme, I would not hand in to her four or five, none of them good.

Mademoiselle reported that my French was fast, but inaccurate. She considered my accent good, she said, but my grammar abominable.

Miss Faulkner pointed out to me this scholastic unevenness when she called me into her office one day to warn me that I might not be allowed to take either a speaking or a dancing part in the school's annual production of a Shakespeare play.

I relayed this information to Mother that night at home, and was already bowed down by the certainty that I would be on the wrong side of the footlights the night of the performance, perhaps allowed to distribute programs. Mother's answer was that I was not to count myself defeated so soon; she and I would wade together into my wobbliest subjects and see if we couldn't, between us, bolster them up.

"We'll call in your father for Algebra," she added, "because I don't consider that I have the mathematical stability of a willow wand. But I can drill you in the others."

She drilled me every night after supper at the dining-room table. The family performances of *The Ring* were discontinued until I should be boosted, if possible, into Shakespeare. We had been in the habit of reviewing together my Latin and Greek assignments, only because she loved the two languages and thought it fun to refresh her memory. But she swung into a memory-refreshing bout with my other subjects, until we were both nearly prostrated with exhaustion.

At first she tried turning me over to Father after she had done with me, but early decided that considering my close to subnormal grasp of Mathematics, I had better work at that while such capacity as I had was at its full strength.

Mother and Father were successful. The day that Miss Faulkner called me again to her office, this time to tell me that my average had come up to the level required, and that I could be in *Midsummer Night's Dream*, I rushed downstairs and telephoned Mother at home and Father at his office. That night we had ice cream with chocolate sauce at supper to mark the occasion.

In my mind's eye I saw myself as Titania, but in the eye of Miss Moulton, our English teacher and dramatic coach, I was a rustic. She cast me as Moonshine, the old man, who gives every evidence of mental senility, by declaiming that,

All that I have to say, is, to tell you that the lanthorn is the moon; I, the man in the moon; this thorn-bush, my thorn-bush; and this dog, my dog.

It was not for this, I told Mother, that I had spent those nights at the dining-room table. She assured me that many actresses preferred a character part to the role of heroine,

"All that I have to say is . . ."

because a character part brought out real acting ability; furthermore, however I felt, I must be a good sport about it. Neither of these palliatives soothed me. I doubted that many actresses were such fools as to prefer a grubby little part to a bespangled Queen of the Fairies. And I thought very little of being a good sport. This was a custom almost as strange to me as curtsying. I was not sure whether it was practiced only in cities, or was an attribute to growing up.

I did know that in Muncie I had shouted my pleasure at winning and at my opponent's losing. I had made such comments as "Yah, yah, I beat and you lost." Or, in reverse, "If you hadn't cheated, I'd have beat." To express any other sentiments seemed to me not being true to oneself. But at Faulkner, in basketball and gym meets, we cheered the loser and deprecated our own win. Though it seemed very silly to me I was learning to join in, and I told Mother that certainly, I would be a good sport about the play.

Two days later I was dazed by the reward of virtue. Miss Moulton told me that because of my progress in dancing I was to have an additional part. I was to be a fairy, one of Titania's train, and in that role I was to do a solo dance that Miss Lee would teach me. I told my family and Hilda that night that I would probably never again have anything so wonderful happen to me. Furthermore, I was to wear a green chiffon costume.

The night of the performance finally arrived. Grandmother and Grandfather Kimbrough came up from Muncie to see it, and Grandmother Wiles from Indianapolis. They had seats together with Mother, Father, Brother, and Hilda on the front row of chairs in the gymnasium, where the play was given. The stage, put up at one end of the room, was a very little distance from them. I made my first entrance as the rustic. My costume was a burlap sack and a rope tied around the waist. My hair was concealed under a wig that represented a bald pate, fringed with dank, straggly gray hair. And Miss Moulton had done such an excellent job with wrinkles, furrows and a gray beard, that for a moment after my entrance, my dear ones in the first row didn't recognize me. I could see them clearly, and the realization that they did not instantly know me was gratifying.

I remembered my lines. I even provoked, on some of them, intentional laughter. I made my exit giddy with satisfaction. Girls who were not in the play were waiting in the wings to help me with the rapid change to the character of the fairy.

A few minutes later I took my place among Titania's attendants, and we made a dazzling entrance. From then on, I whipped from one part to the other, as my two roles demanded. I was the rustic and then the fairy, the rustic and then the fairy, until at last the great moment came for my solo dance.

Draped in the pale green chiffon of my dreams, and to the strains of the Mendelssohn "Midsummer Night" music, played on the gymnasium piano by Miss Burgess, our physical education instructor, I ran on tiptoe to the center of the stage. For this entrance, Miss Burgess played fortissimo, to drown out the creaking and thumping of the boards under my tiptoe. I smiled happily at the audience. This was my moment, and I savored it. I pirouetted, and at that instant heard from the front row the voice of my mother raised in agitation but authority, "Emily," it said, "leave the stage."

I recognized the voice and the authority behind it. For a moment I was engulfed in panic. But on the instant I decided that this was a crisis in which I must make my own decision. Mother had seen my green chiffon costume; it had been made at home under her supervision by a seamstress. If it seemed too flimsy to her now, because my grandparents were there, she would have to suffer. My life must not be ruined. I could hear the music faltering under Miss Burgess's fingers while she awaited my decision. I pirouetted again, put down a determined foot on a second rendering of the first step, and heard my mother's words repeated more forcibly than before. Almost simultaneously I heard from the back of the auditorium a ripple of laughter that increased in volume as I doggedly continued my steps until the abrupt descent of the curtain mercifully cut off the sound.

As I stood staring in helpless rage as the blank folds of material closed down in front of me, my helpers rushed on from the wings. They were giggling. One of them whispered,"I'm awfully sorry." In the exigencies of the rapid changes, they had forgotten to remove the bald wig of the old man, though they had taken off my beard. They remedied their lapse.

I did my dance. At my reappearance the audience clapped enthusiastically, and laughed at the same time.

After the play, when the parents and the cast were being served cookies and cups of lemonade, Miss Moulton came up to our family group and put her arm around me. She smiled at my visitors, and patting my arm, said, "She made a fine rustic, didn't she?"

14. Close to Nature

WHEN FATHER HAD A SLEEPING PORCH ADDED TO OUR apartment on Blackstone Avenue, the other five families in the building were interested. People in the neighborhood, too, whom Mother had never met, came over and asked to see it. Mother didn't tell Father about any of these callers because he was moody about the addition. He said he had thought only a crackpot would build apartment houses with such a thing as a sun parlor sticking out in front of each flat. He had never seen their like until we moved to Chicago from Muncie, Indiana, and it embarrassed him to walk past them. He said he always looked away so that he wouldn't see the poor wretches exposed like animals at the zoo. In Muncie people pulled down their shades at night, and a living room wasn't hung out on the front of the house like a lantern. Now here he was, hanging something like it out the back, only worse, because his was the *only one*.

Mother thought this an inconsistent point of view. She told him it embarrassed her to walk down Main Street in Muncie past the barber shop. She always looked away, she said, to avoid meeting the eye of a man lying back in a chair with lather over his face and only a plate glass window separating her from such intimacy. Besides, a sleeping porch would have the shades pulled down. It would make her feel closer to Muncie, too, not actually to sleep in an apartment, like ants in an ant hill. Father said he had yet to hear of anyone in Muncie who slept on his back porch. Mother's answer was that to get an equivalent amount of purity in a city, you needed to take in more fresh air than in a small town because city air was polluted.

It was not an easy campaign for Mother, but she won it. When Father insisted that the arrival of the milkman would waken him every morning, she printed a sign to be tacked up on the back door. It read, "Milkman: Please tiptoe, and set down bottles quietly. Sleeping. Thank you." When she showed it to Father, he gave up and sent for a carpenter.

The carpenter partitioned off part of the back porch, screened it with window screening and with wide blinds of green and white striped awning material on rollers, like window shades, and he put a door in the partition. The space was large enough for two beds, with very little room between.

Of the whole plan, the door in the partition was the only detail that Father won. Mother wanted a stile over the pantry window that opened on the sleeping porch. She said it was practical because they would not have to go outside from the back door to reach the sleeping compartment and be chilled. She argued further that it was more reasonable to proceed from one room to another than to go from indoors to outdoors to comparative indoors again. Father's answer was: first, that he saw no difference between being chilled all night in your bed outdoors and having a preliminary chill between the back door and the sleeping porch entrance, a total distance of five feet; second, that to introduce as an argument any aspect of reason into a conception so irrational as a sleeping chamber on a back porch was so irrelevant as not to be worth discussing. Mother would not have been downed by being told what was reasonable and what wasn't, but when he pointed out in addition that he weighed 165 pounds and she weighed 98, that the window was twenty inches wide and that it would scrape him, she yielded. She was a little annoyed, she said, that he hadn't mentioned that in the first place. Father murmured that it was hard to know what to mention.

My social standing at Miss Faulkner's School increased appreciably when, unequipped to conjugate the verb *"dor-mir,"* I distracted Mademoiselle by throwing off the information that we were adding a sleeping porch to our apartment. My classmates were charmed; Mademoiselle was distracted but horrified. It was of the madness, she insisted to the class, this desire in America for the fresh air. In France, which was, as all the world knew, a country of reasonable persons, a current of air, even, was not permitted to attack the health. But at the United States, what was passing? Windows, open, open, open. Mademoiselle pushed her arms into the air in successive spurts, to show that the window was opened all the way. And then, what do they do, these Americans, put up a screen across the window? But no. Not at all. They put their heads into it. They permit the winds, the storms, even the tempests—Mademoiselle revolved her arms to indicate a tempest—to enter. And now, even that is not sufficing. They must go outside of their houses to sleep. One could understand it for the sport of the hunting, or for the cause of exploring, but for simply the sleeping—certainly it was not sage.

I repeated this to Mother and Father at dinner that night. Father said hopefully that there was a good deal in what she said. Mother answered that French people, preferring boulevards to nature, seldom were healthy. Her idea of the porch, she insisted, had been born only of her concern for Father's health. Long hours in a stuffy downtown office would sap his strength, and eating in smoky restaurants instead of walking home to dinner (or lunch, as they called it in Chicago) as he used to do in Muncie. But lying close to nature at night would give him renewed strength, like Antaeus. Father said whenever Mother called on the Greeks, he was a goner.

The carpenter finished his work about five o'clock one afternoon early in June, and Mother was so eager to have him gone she helped sweep up all the shavings and pack his tools. She made the beds, too, to show Hilda how easy it was. You moved sideways between them to the foot, where you could turn around and come back, reversed. Hilda stood in the pantry, at the window, to watch the demonstration. Mother said Hilda must also breathe deeply while making the beds. The exercise would then be beneficial and make her think she was back in her native Sweden.

I watched from the pantry doorway to the kitchen, and I could see from the stiffening of Hilda's back that she was not impressed. But Mother came in happily through the window. Hilda stood aside and watched with disapproval when she straddled the sill. I asked if I could tell Father that the porch was ready, and Mother said no, it was to be a surprise for him, that they would sleep outdoors that very night.

"Then I make him some gingerbread," Hilda said, only she pronounced it yinyerbrad. "He likes it. He should have it."

Brother and I hinted about the surprise all through dinner, but Mother didn't tell Father what it was until he was eating gingerbread and applesauce, his favorite dessert. He was surprised. He said the carpenter had promised it wouldn't be finished until some time the following week. Mother agreed that it wouldn't have been, except that she had helped, because she knew Father was going away Sunday night on a business trip. She wanted him to be able to sleep on the porch before he left. It would build up his health for the trip. Hilda was clearing the table, but she brought in the gingerbread again and urged him to have another piece.

Brother and I begged to be allowed to stay up to see Mother and Father in their beds outdoors, but when Father said, why, certainly, and didn't we want to ask some of the neighbors, too, Mother told us we were not to ask such silly things. There was nothing about a sleeping porch that was in the least out of the ordinary. Father told her that he might, if he were allowed, point out one or two things about ours that struck him as out of the ordinary.

The next morning when Brother and I got to the breakfast table, Father had already gone to the office. Mother said he had waked up very early, at sunrise in fact, because she hadn't pulled down the shade on the garden side. She'd been up a long time and seemed tired. Father had roused her at six. I heard her tell Hilda about it. He had cooked breakfast so that Mother would get the spirit of camping. After this, she would pull down all the shades. Hilda said they could do what they pleased about the porch, but that she would leave if she had to start the day with a dirty kitchen.

Things went along without incident for the next few days. Father even admitted one morning at breakfast that he was beginning to like it: the shades were down, the milkman was tiptoeing, he slept until his usual hour. When he woke up, he said he felt as if he were camping, to smell coffee from the kitchen, and that it gave him a roaring appetite. Mother was very pleased. But Sunday morning brought a setback, for which I was partly responsible because of my moths.

There were thirty-eight of them, ten Cecropias, two Lunas, one Emperor, the rest, lesser varieties. Until Sunday they were in their cocoons, and until Saturday the cocoons were in a big box in my room. They had been there all winter except for intermittent inspections. I had gathered them on countryside excursions around Muncie during my Thanksgiving holiday there. I wanted them for my butterfly collection.

Saturday afternoon, about five o'clock, I took them out of the box, spread them along my window sill, went over each one carefully, and saw, with excitement, that they were all beginning to open. The idea of the sleeping porch as a hatching ground visited me at that moment. I went at once to my parents' room to tell them about it, but they asked me not to come in. They were dressing to go to dinner and the theater in town with friends; they were late, the friends were waiting. I wanted very much to show the cocoons to somebody; Brother was out playing, so I fetched Hilda from her room. She only said not to leave the dirty things lying around and went back to her room. I did not mention to her the sleeping porch idea.

As soon as Mother and Father left, I got wire hairpins from Mother's bureau drawer and took the cocoons out to the porch. I attached each one to the screening by running a hairpin through and twisting it around the twig to which the cocoon was attached. I was stringing up the last one when I heard Hilda calling me. I didn't want her to find me there lest she make complications so I went in through the pantry window and didn't answer her until I was well into the dining room. She was looking for me in my room, to tell me that Mrs. Cornwall and Virginia, my school chum, were waiting for me. I had been invited to spend the night at Virginia's house. Hilda asked me where the moths were.

"Put away," I said, grabbed my suitcase from her hands, and ran.

I didn't come home until after Sunday school the next day. On my way out, I stopped to talk to Brother. He stayed on for church because he sang in the choir. I usually stayed, too, and went to church with Mother and Father, but I wanted to get back to my moths. Brother told me to duck around by a secret way we knew and go up the back stairs so as to avoid meeting Mother and Father on their way to church.

"Are the moths out?" I asked.

"You bet your sweet life they are," he said, "and the family's going to settle you."

I got up the back way safely and went straight into the sleeping porch. The moths were beautiful. Most of them were clinging to the screening, but some were on the beds, slowly waving their wings dry, and others were coasting through the air. I yelled to Hilda to come and see them.

"I seen them earlier," she called back, "when I heard your folks holler. I thought I *was* seeing things, too, I tell you." By this time she had come to the window and was leaning over the sill. She shivered at the sight of the beautiful moths.

"Your papa and mama's mad," she added. "Better come in, and I make you some toast with powdered sugar." I knew from the offer that things were pretty bad.

While I ate, she told me what had happened. Mother and Father had come home late, gone to bed and to sleep without turning on the light to read. Mother had left a note for Hilda, saying they were going to sleep until nine o'clock.

But at eight o'clock a trio of musicians had arrived in the back yard.

This little band came every Sunday morning to all the back yards in the neighborhood. One played an accordion, another the harp, and the third was a tenor. The maids liked their music and threw down money, but Mother and Father had never heard them. So when the sound of a harp wakened them, they were surprised. Mother had thought she must be dreaming. Then she had opened her eyes and had seen shapes that moved all up and down the screen. She had closed her eyes again, convinced that she was terribly ill and in a delirium.

Piecing it together afterward at breakfast that Hilda said they didn't eat, Mother and Father decided that, as Mother closed her eyes, Father had wakened to the sound of a harp and opened his eyes on the sights of moths in the air, on the screen, and on his bed. He had then closed his eyes on the conviction that he was dead and had lain in a cold rigidity of horror until a full-voiced attack on "O Sole Mio" from the tenor, with an enthusiastic entry of the accordion, brought him to an open-eyed sitting position, simultaneously with Mother. They had both cried out loudly together their relief at the sight of each other, the realization that they were alive and well, and the creeping horror at what was slithering around and over them. This was what had brought Hilda on the run into the situation.

By the time Mother and Father came home from church, I had put the moths to sleep with gasoline and was ready to mount them. I had plenty of time for the process because I was confined to my room until I went to school on Monday morning. I was also forbidden to go near the sleeping porch at any future time without asking permission and stating my purpose.

My father was discussing the sharpest methods of mayhem.

Father was prepared for the musicians the next Sunday, dressed and waiting for them. He explained about the sleeping porch and asked them to omit this stop on their Sunday tour. They smiled, bowed; Father nodded back at them. Watching over the back porch railing, I was impressed by the ceremony of their departure, hats waving, Father waving back, a little cadenza on the harp before it was slung over the musician's shoulder, and a rondo of expressions of warm friendship as they trudged down the driveway.

The following Sunday morning they were back again. Father, taken by surprise, was not dressed for them. He leaned over the porch railing, expressed his surprise at their return, and explained the situation again. Once more the trio departed with flourishes and returned the next week, and the week after. By this time my father, a mild man, was discussing openly the sharpest methods of mayhem.

"They will drive me stark, raving, gibbering mad," he said, "and I've told them so. They will see me ready for an asylum before they're through."

Sometime during the Saturday night of the following week, Mother woke and heard rain. She put on her bed lamp to make sure the shades were drawn down tight and saw to her dismay that the ceiling had sprung a slight leak. The drops were infrequent but they fell close to Father's head. Mother started to rouse him to move indoors to their bedroom, but he was sleeping so soundly, she couldn't bear to wake him. When she explained this at breakfast on Sunday morning, she repeated several times, "I would have wakened you if it had been a bad leak, but I'm sure a sound sleep with a little leak is much better than being disturbed."

Whatever Father thought of it, this was her reasoning. She slipped out of bed with the intention of creeping through the pantry window and finding in the house something that would make a shield for him. Just on the other side of the window she saw Hilda's bright red umbrella, opened and set on the pantry floor to dry. Mother reached for it pulled it over to her, closed, and drew it through the window. She opened it again quietly and arranged it behind Father's head, tucking the handle down the side of the bed next the screening. Just about to settle down again, she thought that since the umbrella had been used, it was damp. The dampness so near him might make Father catch cold. She returned to the pantry window, leaned far in, and was able to reach, by stretching, the drawer in which Hilda's clean ruffled white dust caps were kept. She withdrew one of these and very carefully placed it on father's head. Her later recital made this very clear.

At eight o'clock the musicians arrived. The rain had stopped, the sun was out, Father was sound asleep. At the first note he woke with a cry of rage. He flung up the shade and rose to his knees, full-panoplied in the ruffled dust cap, somewhat down over one eye, the scarlet umbrella coquettishly over his shoulder, his angry face pressed against the screen, and he shouted above all the music. The trio stopped in the middle of a bar, Mother said. She heard the tenor take a note higher than she would have believed possible. Then they were gone. Father reported to Mother that the tenor got tangled in the harp and the accordion. Father was inordinately pleased about it until he discovered his own accouterments. He would not sleep on the porch after that if the weather report even said, "possible showers," though Mother had the roof fixed immediately. The musicians never came back.

We went away for the rest of the summer. Father only stayed with us for two weeks and after that for the week ends. But we had Hilda with us, so the apartment was closed and Father lived at a hotel in town. It was well into October before Mother persuaded him to accept the sleeping porch again. He argued that the weather would soon be too cold for outdoor sleeping and that it was a pity to resume a habit that could only be temporary. Mother surprised him with the news that she had bought flannel nightclothes for them both, and two soapstones. She had been reading articles about outdoor sleeping and learned, she said, how to accomplish it and how particularly beneficial it was. You not only did not catch cold on a sleeping porch; you didn't catch cold anywhere all winter. Father prophesied that they probably wouldn't catch anything so trivial as a cold; they'd skip right over into double pneumonia.

Grandmother Wiles came from Indianapolis for my birthday on the twenty-third of October. She was on her way to California for the winter and planned to spend a few days with us en route. It was her first visit and the first time she had been in any apartment. She was delighted with ours, especially with the accessibility of the kitchen, she said. We didn't understand that, because a kitchen was on the other side of a dining room in a house just the same as in an apartment. Not in her house, she said. In her house there were pantries between; in our apartment the pantry was beyond and to one side of the kitchen. She insisted that it made a very great difference. In Indianapolis she had no familiarity with the room. Here she could see a little of it when the swing door to the dining room opened. Cozy and warm, it reminded her of the kitchen in an uncle's farm she had visited as a child. She suggested that she might read her morning paper there in the rocking chair by the radiator.

Hilda was serving when Grandmother suggested this and

shook her head violently, over Grandmother's head, at
Mother. I saw her, but Grandmother didn't, and I saw
Mother nod reassuringly to Hilda. Mother didn't often
obstruct Grandmother's plans. Nobody did. Father said that
the song, "I want what I want when I want it," had been
written about her, but Mother denied this, and told Brother
and me that Father didn't mean it. I wondered how Mother
was going to prevent Grandmother's reading in the kitchen
if Grandmother said she was going to. I knew, however, that
Mother was going to try, because Hilda shaking her head
meant that she would leave if Grandmother invaded her
kitchen. The whole matter was settled in a little more than
twenty-four hours.

Grandmother arrived in the late afternoon, the day before my birthday. We all went to meet her at the Englewood Station. As soon as she had taken off her hat, sealskin
jacket, kid gloves, and blown into the gloves so that they
would hold their shape, she inspected the apartment. At
dinner that night she told her plan about using the kitchen
because she liked it so much. At bedtime she went out to
see Hilda heat the soapstones for the porch and wrap them
in layers of old blanketing.

Mother had written her all about the sleeping porch, and
Grandmother had approved enthusiastically. She generally
approved anything that was out of the ordinary pattern.
When she said good night to Mother, I heard her say how
pleasant the kitchen was when she had been out with Hilda,
warm and cozy.

The next morning after breakfast Grandmother picked
up the *Chicago Tribune* from the dining room table and
headed for the kitchen. Mother said quickly that my whole
class was coming for dinner to celebrate my birthday, and
she asked Grandmother please to go with her to get favors

and odds and ends for the party. When I left for school, Grandmother had on her hat and sealskin jacket and was putting on her kid gloves, one finger at a time, wetting the thumb and forefinger of the other hand to push the tight kid down. Mother's method for keeping her out of the kitchen had been successful, but I wasn't going to have a birthday every day, and Mother didn't go out so early as that every morning to do errands. I thought that something else would have to happen.

The birthday party was fine. We had creamed chicken and peas, hot rolls and mashed potatoes, ice cream in a spun sugar basket, and a chocolate birthday cake that Hilda made. There was candy in a fluted pink paper cup in front of each plate. Everyone brought me a present. The whole affair was to my liking except that the guests had to go home at eight o'clock because it was a school night. I was allowed to stay up until nine since it was my birthday. Bedtime ordinarily was at eight-thirty sharp, including light turned out and window open, so the nine o'clock dissipation was almost the most heady feature of the whole day.

Mother said she was going to bed too, at the same time. She was completely exhausted. Father told her he would be along shortly. He was going to read a little longer. Grandmother went to her room to go to bed, we thought.

It took us a long time to straighten out in sequence the incidents that followed. I came in only at the end when there was a great deal of confusion, but I think it was this way:

Grandmother undressed and put on her dressing gown. By that time she thought Father had gone to bed on the porch because the lights in the living room were out. Actually, he had undressed but was reading, in his dressing gown, on the couch in the front bedroom. He didn't like to read on the porch because his hands got too cold, and he wouldn't wear mittens like Mother. Grandmother went into the living room and got the evening paper. Thinking Mother and Father safely on the porch, she proceeded down the hall to the kitchen and settled herself happily in the rocking chair by the radiator, just as she had intended since the afternoon of the preceding day.

But Mother was not asleep; she was trying to make up her mind to leave her soapstone-warmed bed for extra blankets from the linen closet. A slight noise in the kitchen seemed the answer to her dilemma. She thought it was Father on his way to the porch. So she threw off the covers, edged to the pantry window on her knees, leaned over the sill, and called loud enough to reach him through the closed pantry door, "Hal, Hal, will you bring—?"

That was as far as she got. Grandmother, reading placidly and triumphantly in the rocking chair, gave a piercing scream of astonishment, started back involuntarily, and the rocking chair turned over on top of her. She struck her head against the radiator and was knocked out.

Mother, jarred by this scream in the dead of night, and not ten feet away from her, screamed back and jumped with fright. The jump brought her chin down on the window sill so hard her chin was cut. It started to bleed. Father, coming quietly through the dining room on his way to the porch, heard both screams, pushed the swing door to the kitchen, and roared through so fast that the door, swinging back with double speed and violence from his impact, struck him in the forehead. He came staggering into the kitchen, roaring, "Get out of here!" He thought a burglar was in the kitchen. At the moment he was staggering about, holding his forehead, roaring at the burglar, Mother climbed over the window sill and ran into the kitchen. At almost the same moment Hilda opened the door from her room, and Brother and I reached the kitchen from our rooms. We were the first to see Mother holding her hand cupped under her chin and blood dripping between her fingers. She said, "I'm all right. Where's Mother?"

Father said, "Your MOTHER? Where would she be? She's in bed. Where's the burglar?"

But Hilda pointed to the rocking chair upside down, and we saw Grandmother's feet sticking out from under it. Grandmother was a very majestic woman, and it was strange to see her like that.

Father and Hilda carried her to her bed while Mother telephoned Dr. Black. Grandmother came round all right, but Dr. Black had to take two stitches in her scalp, and he was the first person to notice the big lump on Father's head where the swing door had hit him. He put a compress on that, with adhesive tape, and he taped Mother's chin after he had stopped the bleeding and decided it didn't need stitches. Mother was distressed that she hadn't noticed Father's head, and Father was upset about that, too. He said he thought he might have a concussion, but Dr. Black said he didn't.

When Grandmother was coming to, she said, "How do you do, Doctor, I must show you the kitchen. Charming place. Very cozy for reading." After that she went to sleep because Dr. Black gave her something.

She left for California a few days after that. She was still wearing a bandage, and some of her hair had been shaved off for it. But she hadn't gone back to the kitchen except to say good-by to Hilda.

Father *never* went back to the sleeping porch so Mother gave it up, too. It was turned into a play room for Brother and me, but nobody slept there again.

15. Mary Garden's Carmen, and Brother's

BROTHER'S PRODUCTION OF *Carmen* WAS INTRODUCED IN our back yard on a Saturday morning, one week after the *Carmen* of Mary Garden that our parents took us to see at the Auditorium. It was near the end of the opera season and an early spring that year in Chicago. Our jonquils and narcissus were in bloom, the tulips had budded, even the peony shoots were well up, and the apple tree by the garage was a pale pink mist of opening blossoms.

The fact that our apartment had a back yard and a garden made it different from other city dwellings, Mother wrote in her letters back to Muncie. The building was owned by an elderly bachelor and his very old mother, Mrs. Eisenman. They were Germans and our next-door neighbors to the north. Theirs was an old house by Chicago counting, red brick with an iron fence around it. Our building stood on what had been the garden. When it was built, Mrs. Eisenman had insisted that the borders be left for the tenants. She had planted for herself, at the same time, a small garden behind the brick house. Her gardener, John, took care both of that one and ours. She would direct him from her bedroom window, tapping on the pane to catch his attention and indicating by elaborate pantomime, what she wanted him to do. My bedroom window on the third floor looked down on hers. I liked to watch these conferences. Occasionally, when pantomime failed to communicate her orders, she would open the window and call instructions in a high, quavering voice or very politely request Brother and his companions, Lily and Rudy, not to play ball near our flowerbeds.

On the Saturday of the Mary Garden opera, Mother, Brother, and I came out of our apartment at about eleven o'clock. Gus was sweeping the driveway so we knew that John was working in our garden. Whenever John came over to our yard, Gus came out of the cellar and swept the driveway. Mother said she didn't know whether this was an evidence of suspicion since they never talked to each other, or of sociability, because with Swedish people it was hard to tell. Gus was Swedish.

Mother said good morning to Gus and called to John that his flowers made her believe there was spring in a big city. Brother shouted at them both that we had to catch the Illinois Central train to town because we were going to a grand opera. John called back, "That's right," to Mother and "That's fine," to Brother.

Gus didn't say anything. We hadn't expected that he would. Gus only talked to Lily. He had pale blue eyes, and his skin and sparse hair were almost the same color. They both looked dusty. Rudy looked like his father. But Lily's hair was the color of the yellow-red nasturtiums along our fence. Mother had pointed to them one day and said to Father, "There's the color of Lily Stonewall's hair. You can't call that flax, unless it's flax on fire." Mother also called her eyes Delft blue.

Every day when Lily came up the drive on her way home from school, Gus would be waiting outside the entrance to their basement apartment. I got home about the same time, and I would see him rub his dirty cracked hand back and forth over the top of her head. He always said, "How was it at school today? You was a smart girl, huh?"

She would duck under his hand and run down the steps. He never bothered to speak to Rudy or to us. Sometimes Mother got a word out of him, but not the morning we went to *Carmen*.

At the foot of our driveway Mother waved toward Mrs. Eisenman's window. She told us to wave, too, and I saw old Mrs. Eisenman standing there, shaking a little white hand-kerchief at us. Brother cupped his hands around his mouth and roared so loud everybody in our building must have heard, "We're going to *Carmen*. It's grand opera. And eat at the Congress Hotel."

Mrs. Eisenman nodded her head rapidly and put her finger to her lips. Mother jerked Brother's hands from his face.

"Hush, Brother," she said. "Mrs. Eisenman knows. I had tea with her yesterday. That's why she was watching for us."

I felt it was not worth her while to look for us since I was not wearing my spring outfit, and I told Mother so. She had decided at the last minute it might get very chilly by the time we came home and told me to change back to my old gray winter coat. Even unbuttoned, it made me sweat. As we walked along, I directed Mother's hand around inside the velvet collar to see how wet my neck was, and I reminded her I was bound to get a heat rash from the sweat and the elastic under my chin. My hat was beaver. That was making my head sweat, too, and the elastic was as stiff as a board from sucking it all winter. It was even tied in a knot with a big loop under my chin to take up the slack because there was no more stretch in it. I showed it to her.

Mother said, "I don't want to have to tell you again, Emily. Spring weather is treacherous. Lots of little girls would be so excited about going to see a real opera, they wouldn't know whether they had on a coat and hat or not."

"Who?" I asked.

"Would you prefer to go home right now?" Mother inquired.

I did not speak again all the way in town.

Brother talked without stopping.

Father met us in the lobby of the Congress Hotel. He said he had engaged a table by the window so that we could look right out on Michigan Avenue. I began to feel less dour about the day, though the weather had not cooled as yet and I was still sweating. Still, I had eaten downtown once before at the Tip Top Inn in the Mother Goose Room, and Brother had never eaten downtown, nor at a hotel except in the children's dining room at the Del Prado. This gave me a superiority that I explained to him, and I began to feel gay. But he was then told he could order anything he wanted to eat, since this was an occasion we were not to forget, and he asked the waiter for alligator pear salad, chocolate ice cream, a peanut butter sandwich, and baked beans. He also explained to the waiter he much preferred baked beans out of a can to the ones cooked at home—Van Camp's if they happened to have that kind. I asked at once to be taken home. The day was irrevocably ruined as far as I was concerned. Mother said briskly my idea was a good one, since I seemed bent on spoiling the day for every-

one else, but it was impractical because no one was going
to sacrifice a wonderful treat like this to take me home. So
would I please straighten myself out immediately? I did not
speak again throughout the meal.

A tunnel connected the Congress Hotel with the Auditorium. Brother said it was probably a secret tunnel that
was a hideout for smugglers, but Father said everyone who
went to the opera here knew about it. I could see Brother
was disappointed by this, and that pleased me, but he proceeded to try the echo by slapping his hand against his
mouth in a loud Indian war whoop. I said I would sit down
right there in the tunnel and wait for them to come back
after the opera. Mother answered it would be a great pity if
I did because I would miss walking through at the same
time as Madame Schumann-Heink, and pointed to her just
ahead.

If my mother had said Madame Schumann-Heink was
circling about over our heads, I would not have been more
astonished. I had been taken to hear her in a concert at
Petty's Skating Rink in Muncie, and Grandfather had records of hers on his Victrola, along with Scotti, Caruso, and
Nordica. I hadn't supposed such people as they ever walked
at all. I thought they were borne from place to place in
special carriages like chariots. But there she was, walking,
and not even like a queen. She was hurrying. I moved
quickly ahead of my family and went abreast of her the rest
of the way, but I pretended I didn't know she was there.

In the lobby of the Auditorium my father made me
rejoin them and stay close to him. I didn't mind. Spiritually
I was still with Madame Schumann-Heink and happy,
though I walked in with Mother. Father followed us, holding Brother by the hand. I had forgotten that Brother was
with us; in my mind, Madame Schumann-Heink was asking

me if I would like to go home with her after the opera because she had noticed me in the tunnel, and thought how beautiful I was, and that undoubtedly I had a wonderful voice. Then she asked me to go abroad with her to study, and after that I became the most famous singer in the world. Brother called ahead to Mother, could we see the sideshows afterward and could he have some crackerjack now? Several people near us laughed, and I fell dead immediately, at Madame Schumann-Heink's feet, by my own hand, preferring to die, young as I was, than to live in constant shame and dishonor. Father pushed me past the man who was collecting tickets.

Our seats were in the front row of the balcony. After several tries Mother decided on a seating arrangement of Brother first, then herself, then me, and my father on the aisle. She offered me her opera glasses, and I stretched over the rail, holding them to my eyes, to shut off my alien companions and to find my dear friend and benefactor, Madame Schumann-Heink. Mother leaned across my back to talk to Father, and Brother was obliterated. Therefore, we were all happy for a moment, until something went across the exposed end of my opera glasses, and I very nearly went over the rail. It turned out to be a glider that Brother had made from one of the pages of his program and not the first one he had launched. Mother took away his program and his reserve supply, but before I could crack him with the opera glasses, the lights dimmed, and she told us to watch for the conductor to come through the orchestra.

What we saw on the stage that afternoon was very difficult to connect with the refined version of *Carmen* that Mother had told us. In the first place she had made a bullfight the main theme. Carmen she had portrayed to us as a young, high-spirited bullfight enthusiast. Since it seemed to

me unlikely that a bullfight was going to take place in the
mountain fastnesses, I could not figure out what Carmen
was doing there. My own approach to it did not clarify the
story. In uneasy anticipation of an imminent entrance of
bulls, I kept my hands over my face or ears a good portion of
the time. But on the whole, I was pleased with the opera.

Brother lost interest in the last act. Up to then he had
stood, the upper part of his body across the broad plush
rail, his elbows on its far side, his chin between his two
hands. He lost interest because he thought the bullfight was
going on behind the backdrop. Arriving at this conclusion,
he began instantly to climb over Mother and me and Father
in order to get downstairs and around to where the fighting
was. Restrained from this and thrust back into his seat,
with Mother whispering in his ear that he was mistaken and
people all around hushing them both, he slid down so that
he could put his feet on the railing and didn't look at the
stage again. He also withdrew from us into a total silence
that lasted all the way home—a happy circumstance, but
Mother complained about it on the Illinois Central train
where she and Father and I sat together, Brother by himself
across the aisle.

"I don't know whether he enjoyed it or not," she said. "I
never know what he enjoys. He talks enough as long as he's
on his regular schedule. But expose him to anything new,
and when he's seen it, he retreats like a Trappist monk."

I thought this reference had something to do with the
fur trade, and the rest of the way home happily pictured
Brother retreating into the frozen wastes, trapping.

As soon as we reached our driveway, Brother muttered
he had something very important to discuss with Rudy
Stonewall and disappeared down the outside cellar steps.
When Mother rapped three times on the radiator pipe with

the heel of her slipper, he came up to dinner, but he didn't talk.

All the following week I talked considerably, at school about my friendship with Madame Schumann-Heink and at home about *Carmen*. But Brother didn't mention the day.

The following Saturday morning, however, he conducted the Blackstone Avenue performance of the opera. I think it was about half-past eleven when I heard the overture. At the time I thought it was only the regular Saturday-morning wrangling among Brother and his chums, assembled in our back yard. But Hilda came into my room where I was lying on my bed reading, and said, "The boys are up to something down there. You better go see. Your mother's out."

I followed her to the back porch and looked over the railing.

All the boys—there were ten or so that morning—had formed a restless circle around Lily. She wore a striped wool afghan like an Indian blanket over her middy blouse and skirt. My grandmother Wiles had crocheted the afghan and it was usually across the foot of a couch in Mother's room. Lily held the ends of it in one fist across her chest, so tight her thick yellow braids were pushed up in the air by its fold across her back. She carried a jonquil in her other hand. John must have given it to her. Children weren't allowed to pick the flowers, but John was working at the jonquil bed. Gus was sweeping the driveway.

Lily pushed through the boys and went over to a chair that lay on its side at one end of the yard, with a small Oriental prayer rug thrown over it. The chair belonged to Gus. He kept it against the cellar steps. The prayer rug came from our vestibule. Lily squatted down behind the chair, rested her chin on its edge, and stared glumly at Brother.

"Now," Brother said, "that's right. You're Carmen, and you watch me fight the bull. When I come in you pretend to throw flowers over the rail of your box, and you shout 'Hola!' and wave your shawl. Put the flower between your teeth."

Lily bit down hard on the jonquil, but she didn't say anything.

Brother turned back to the boys.

"Now then," he told them, "Rudy, you lead the smugglers and try to stop me fighting. The rest of you are my friends and you try to keep them from stopping me. I'm busy with the bull. But first you march in with me all around the arena. I'm the leader. Rudy and I draw sides."

There was some scuffling and bickering over who were going to be bullfighters and who smugglers. Brother yelled, "Come on, if you're going to."

They drew off in two teams. Brother and his team went to the driveway, and Rudy took his to the far side of the yard, around the corner of the building. Brother adjusted a baseball cap sideways across his head and threw, over his left shoulder and outstretched arm, Mother's golf cape, with the red plaid lining on the outside. He took a deep breath and let it out in a roaring opening of the Toreador Song. He sang alto in St. Paul's church choir, but he could also produce another voice with the volume and quality of the horn on a Lake Michigan ore boat. He marched into the ring, leading with this voice, the other bullfighters in formation behind him. In front of Carmen's box he swept off his cap, placed it over his heart and bowed low. He stopped singing long enough to give her a snappy direction.

"Shout HOLA."

Before he could get into his horn voice again, which always required a deep breath in preparation, Lily let go her afghan and jumped over her box. She stood directly in front of him and opened her mouth wide. A thundering roar came out of it, almost as good as my brother's, and, simultaneously, tears flooded her cheeks and chin. That was the way she always cried. She never seemed to need any preparation.

Gus got to her while Brother was letting out his breath and staring at her. He grabbed Brother's shoulder and shook him.

"You swat Lily?" he asked.

"No, I didn't," Brother said in jerks, because Gus was shaking him.

Lily gave another roar, this time with words in it. I couldn't hear what they were, but Gus stopped shaking my brother and crouched down close to her face to try to make them out.

My brother answered them.

"You *can't* be a bullfighter, Lily. Bullfighters are *men*."

Gus rose and looked down at my brother. The smugglers had come out from their hiding place. All the boys were crowded around Gus and my brother and Lily.

"She don't want to be no *bullfighter*," Gus said. "She want to be the BULL." He scowled at the whole Carmen company. "And she's goin' to *be* the bull, or else you boys clear out of my yard, *all* of you."

The company took this in silence, but they all looked to Brother. He spoke for them.

"Listen, Gus, this is *Carmen*. You know, that I went to see. I told you. Well, you got to have a Carmen or you can't play it. That's the name of the whole opera. Lily's the Carmen."

Lily roared again. "Bull," she said, and the tears squirted down her face.

Gus looked at her anxiously, running his prickly hand

Lily bent over from the waist and said, "Moo."

up and down her hair. Then he took a big, dark blue handkerchief out of his overalls pocket and wiped off her face. He stuffed it back in his pocket and announced his decision.

"Lily is Bull."

Lily closed her mouth and smiled happily.

The boys muttered in disgust and my brother said all right, the game was over. They all started to walk away. Lily looked up at her father and opened her mouth again.

Gus spoke, the quickest I ever heard him.

"I'm the Carmen."

Before the boys could doubt him, he walked behind the chair, picked up the afghan, hitched it around his shoulders, squatted down on his haunches, and put the jonquil between his teeth, only like a pipe.

Lily wiped her hand across her cheeks and under her nose, walked to the middle of the yard, bent over from the waist, smiled at my brother and said, "Mooooo."

The smugglers, the bullfighters, and Brother accepted it. They returned to their places. My brother took a deep breath, let it out with the Toreador Song in the boat-horn voice, and led the bullfighter's parade into the arena again. He stopped at Carmen's box and bowed uncertainly. Gus nodded his head several times, the jonquil bobbing up and down between his teeth, and waved his hand to return the greeting.

The procession continued around the yard. When it had made the circle, Brother said, "Halt." He pulled off Mother's golf cape, began waving it in front of him and moved toward Lily in a kind of crouch. When he was within about three feet of her, she jumped at him and hit him in the stomach with her head. He sat down hard and made a sound like his lake-boat voice only lower.

Lily stepped back, smiling at him. Brother stood up, and

so did Gus. Brother said, his arms across his stomach,
"You're not supposed to fight. There wasn't any bull on the
stage, like I told you. I just act out how it's going to be."

Gus spat out the jonquil and shouted, "Get him, Lily.
Fine bull."

The other bullfighters were going to rush Lily, I think,
but the smugglers had sneaked up on them. The smugglers
jumped the bullfighters and Lily came at Brother. He tried
to throw the golf cape over her head. Gus shuffled his feet
and roared, "Bull him, Lily."

All the boys yelled at each other.

Lily bellowed, "Moo."

Brother made his boat voice.

Just about then, I think, my father and the other men
who lived in the building came into the yard from the driveway. They always took the same train out on Saturday, and
I think when they neared home, they had heard the noise in
the back. The first I knew they were there was when Lily
had Brother on the run. She was chasing him around the
yard, and every time she caught up with him, she'd butt
him in the rear and he'd go down, tangled up in the golf
cape. This put him at a disadvantage.

He was getting up from one of these downs, and Lily was
waiting, smiling at him, when Father bellowed, "Tackle
her—round the knees."

That was when I looked over and saw him and the other
men. They began to cheer and slap their folded newspapers
on the palms of their hands. John cheered and waved his
rake.

Brother got up and started off around the arena again,
waving his cape back over his head at Lily. She kept right
behind him.

I didn't think he had heard what Father said, so I yelled, too, "Tackle her. Round the knees."

He heard. He put on speed, then stopped, and whirled around so fast his face pushed into hers. He grabbed her around the neck, though, not the knees. He thought of her as a bull, I'm sure, and so he threw her. He could never have done it if she hadn't been taken by surprise because she was stronger than any of the boys. But she went down, pulling Brother with her, into the jonquil bed.

It was too bad it happened there and when John was working. If he said anything, I couldn't hear it, but I saw him bring the handle of his rake down hard, across Brother's back. I went down the three flights of stairs faster than I ever did it again. When I got to the bottom, I hadn't missed much. My father had just got across the yard, but Gus had reached Brother and Lily ahead of him. He grabbed Brother by the back of his shirt and seat of his pants, lifted him up, and threw him. Brother landed in another part of the bed.

Father gave Gus a big shove in order to get to Brother. Gus, bending over to pick up Lily, lost his balance and went down flat, beside her.

From the moment Brother and Lily went into the jonquils, every bit of yelling stopped. The boys stood in a huddle in the middle of the yard. Brother and Lily didn't cry. It was so quiet I could hear Mrs. Eisenman beating a wild tattoo on her window pane.

Then John said, "You big dumb Swede. You and your Lily—both of you—dumb Swedes."

Gus jumped up and hit John in the nose with his fist, and John sat down. His nose started to bleed in big drops. Gus stooped over and shook his fist back and forth at the tip of John's nose while John was trying to get his handkerchief out of his pocket. Gus said to him very loud, "You never put your foot in this yard again. You go to hell."

I think that was when Mother came back from the lecture she'd been to. I was looking at Gus and John, and at Daddy getting Brother and Lily out of the flowerbed. There wasn't anything left of the jonquils.

I heard Mother say, "Merciful heavens."

Gus heard her, too. He walked away from John to where she was coming across the yard. Everybody stepped back for him. He stopped in front of her and said, "You keep your boy out of my way. Is no good for me, with his ideas."

He didn't even wait for Lily. He jerked his thumb back over his shoulder toward John, sitting on the ground.

"Was my best friend," he said, and moved off toward the cellar steps, down to his flat.

16. *Our Waverly**

A YEAR AFTER WE HAD MOVED TO BLACKSTONE AVENUE, my father bought an electric for Mother. It was a Waverly like the one Grandmother Kimbrough had in Muncie, Indiana. Grandmother didn't drive her Waverly, but Grandfather did, and said that he found it more satisfactory in many ways than his Pierce Arrow, which Hubert drove. Grandfather had sold the horses, Maude and Prince, when he bought the Pierce Arrow, and promoted the hired man, Hubert, from driving them to driving the Pierce Arrow.

Grandmother felt that Hubert's promotion took place too rapidly. It made her uneasy, she told Grandfather, to see Hubert rise and pull far back whenever he put on the brake. Other people she saw driving automobiles didn't do that. Grandfather considered this an unfair criticism. He said it was just a reflex action due to the facts that Prince had had a hard mouth and Maude had been congenitally indifferent. In Grandmother's voluble opinion, it made her nervous, whatever it was.

The Waverly, however, suited them both to a T, particu-

* This chapter first appeared in *The New Yorker*, September 16, 1950.

larly when touring, because Grandfather had the front seat removed. Since the Waverly was operated from the back seat, and entirely by hand, he could stretch his legs at full length while he drove. Grandmother's legs did not reach so far as his, so he put their two suitcases in front of her when they motored over to Wilmington, Ohio, to see his brother, Jervis, and Jervis's wife, my great aunt, Wilmina.

The distance to Wilmington from Muncie is about one hundred and twenty miles, and the Waverly would get them, on one charge, to Dayton, eighty-two miles. This was as far as Grandmother and Grandfather cared to go in one day. They would spend a comfortable night in the hotel there, have the electric recharged, and arrive in Wilmington by the following afternoon.

The maximum speed of the Waverly was thirty-two miles an hour; as fast, Grandfather said, as anyone who was not a fool cared to travel. He reserved twenty-five for emergency spurts, and held generally to a cruising speed of eighteen to twenty.

They rolled along at that pace over the flat, dusty roads of Indiana and the gentle hills of Ohio. Grandmother crocheted, and sometimes read aloud to him, though when she read he had to slow down to twelve. Going faster than twelve made her sick at her stomach if she read, she said, but it was all right for crocheting. Grandfather, leaning back, his legs stretched out, or crossed in front of him, smoked a cigar.

The Waverly was the only place, he declared, where he could sit and smoke in peace, and that further endeared the machine to him. When he smoked at home, Grandmother always came in with a folded newspaper which she waved around the room and around him, blowing gustily at the same time, and making such a strong draft at the back of his neck he had to tuck a large silk handkerchief around his collar when he took out a cigar. She did this even in his own den, an invasion that never failed to rouse him to incredulous and angry surprise. A den was a place to which a man retreated in order to smoke, wasn't it? Grandmother's answer never changed. The smoke settled in the curtains unless you drove it out—no matter *what* the room was for. But in the Waverly she let him smoke peacefully, so long as he kept the window beside him open a little—not too much on account of her neuralgia and his own tendency to a stiff neck.

When farmers hailed them along the road, Grandfather usually stopped the electric for conversation. He was grateful to them for this evidence of friendliness. It distressed him to have them throw stones at the Pierce Arrow and distressed Grandmother to the point of refusing to ride into the country in it. The farmers were doing their best to get gasoline automobiles off the road because they caused so much damage by frightening the horses into runaways.

An electric in the country was a rarity, but the farmers approved of it—thought it a fine way to travel, they told Grandfather, without tormenting horses or folks. Grandfather used this testimony in the letters he wrote us advocating the machine. "The farmer can teach us many things," he said.

In spite of his recommendation, however, my parents did not settle on a Waverly until we had looked over other makes.

The first one we tried was a Detroit. One Monday afternoon a man brought this machine for a demonstration. He went first to my father's office and drove him out. He said the electric took very little more time than the train—they just came spinning along very smoothly.

The demonstrator was pleased. He took us all for a ride in different combinations. Five could ride at one time, but it was crowded. When I rode with Mother he showed her how it was driven.

There were two parallel metal bars, one shorter than the other. They stood upright at the left of the driver and out of his way when he got in and out of the machine. The driver's place was on the left side of the back seat. The demonstrator showed Mother how the rods came down, as simply as closing the lid of a box, because they were each on a hinge. Brought down by a touch, they extended across in front of the driver, one above the other. The longer one was for steering, the shorter for speed control. If you wished to turn left, you pushed the long bar away, or pulled it toward you to turn right. Pushing the shorter bar away would send the machine from first, through the notches of higher speeds, to fifth. Before it would start, however, you had to insert a thick, flat key in a slot. This would turn on the current.

While the demonstrator explained all this, I could see Mother growing restless. Finally, he asked if she would like to try just sitting in the driving seat, and manipulating the speed and steering bars; he would get out, come round to the other side and sit beside her. He opened the door as he was speaking. Mother was in the driver's seat before he had uttered the last syllable.

I sat diagonally across from her on the front seat that ran the full width of the machine. I knew she was not going to let the man get in on the other side; she had had enough of him, and I had a feeling she was going to do more than manipulate the bars. She did—so fast that I hadn't time to brace myself, and was knocked to the floor instantly by the abruptness of our departure. I wasn't hurt, but I stayed where I was until we stopped. We didn't go very far, but we went fast. When I raised up, I saw that we had come out the driveway, across the street, over the curb and the sidewalk between two trees, and were in front of the iron gate to the Stephens' house. Mrs. Stephens, and her son, Jack, were on their front porch trying to open the screen door and get into the house. Mother called through the car window to them, "I've found the brake."

When Father arrived, with the demonstrator and Brother just behind him, Mother explained how it had been her intention to turn left at the foot of the driveway, but instead of the steering, she had pushed the speed bar away from her. She told the demonstrator that perhaps he hadn't sufficiently emphasized the difference between the two bars. He was walking around the electric while she said this, looking, I think, for signs of damage. He seemed to be surprised at the way we had come between the trees without hitting either of them, or scratching the paint on the electric. He only said if Mother would turn the electric over to him, he would try to back it into the street. She and I returned on foot with Father and Brother.

When we reached the curb in front of our building, Father sat down on it. He felt weak, he said. Mother patted his shoulder, but she was preoccupied, and presently she walked away. Brother and I sat down beside Father.

It took the demonstrator a considerable time to retrace the distance Mother had driven in almost nothing, and he scraped a fender against one of the trees that she had cleared nicely. When he did draw up in our driveway again, Mother rejoined us. She had been thinking about the machine, she said, and had decided it was badly designed. She urged the demonstrator to have the company produce a model with a wheel for steering. A wheel was the normal appurtenance;

the very sight of it indicated its purpose. The demonstrator told her few, if any, electrics were made with a real steering wheel, because a wheel took up too much room.

Mother described for him Mrs. Frank Ball's electric in Muncie, made to order for her and the five Ball children. There were three rows of seats in it and the steering apparatus was a wheel, only set flat, like a motorman's. The car was open, too, like a summer trolley. It had proved most satisfactory.

Father suggested from the curb that before she had a special electric built, we investigate other makes, and the demonstrator took his Detroit back downtown.

The next make we tried was an Ohio. Another demonstrator brought one around the next day. It also had a steering bar, but the speed control was a round knob the size of a door knob. It was above and to the left of the steering bar and you revolved it in your left hand to move from one speed notch to the next. Mother was glad to try the machine. She said it was like being thrown from a horse; you had to ride again immediately or you never would; and she insisted that I go too, for the same reason. But she was not relaxed, which was perhaps the reason she tried to revolve the steering bar with her right hand while she was making the rotating motion with her left hand to advance the speed. She was cautious, too. She advanced only to first, then retreated to neutral, then came up to first again. We alternately jerked forward, coasted, jerked forward, coasted, while Mother echoed on the steering bar each rotation of the speed knob. When we had lurched to the corner of the next cross street, Mother stopped the machine and got out. She made me get out, too.

She talked from the curb to the demonstrator, describing the steering wheel on Mrs. Frank Ball's electric, and recommending its adoption by the manufacturers of the Ohio. The demonstrator said he would tell them, but he urged her to try once more the mechanism already on the machine. Once she got used to it, he promised, she would never be bothered again. Mother told him that after practice one could also become skilled in patting the head and rubbing the stomach, but she felt there were other activities more rewarding of that concentration. This disposed of the Ohio.

One afternoon a few days later a demonstrator brought a Waverly for a demonstration. She liked it the minute she saw it. She had never driven Grandmother's, but she said she was sure anyone could drive a Waverly without previous experience, and without confusion, because the speed control was an upright, short lever at the left hand side of the driver, and low down, at about the level of the seat itself. There was nothing else in that same zone, Mother pointed out to the demonstrator, except a small lever into which the key fitted, and which, after unlocking, you set into backward or forward gear as needed. It suggested, she said, the throttle on a locomotive. The steering rod broke at a hinge, like the two rods on the Detroit, to lie across the front of the driver, somewhat like the safety strap in a baby coach. You pushed it away to turn left, pulled it toward you to turn right. There was a foot brake, and you could also brake by pulling back on the speed lever, the demonstrator said. Neither brake should be operated when you were in gear or you would burn out the motor.

Father was at his office when the Waverly arrived. After the man had driven Mother and Brother and me around the neighborhood and given Mother a turn at the controls, he suggested that he drive Mother in town, pick up Father, and bring them both back. Mother was exhilarated by her success with this machine and the demonstrator's insistence that she was the quickest to catch on of all the women he had ever taught. She said she thought she could handle a Waverly without any further help—except perhaps in the downtown traffic—but she made my brother and me get out.

We waved good-by from the sidewalk, but Mother didn't take her hand off the bar to wave back. She nodded several times instead, looking straight ahead of her.

When Mother and Father returned home Brother and I were at the living-room windows watching for them. We had been there such a long time that it was dark. Our parents seemed to be all right when they got out in the driveway, and the Waverly, as well as we could see from the street light, seemed all right, too. The demonstrator drove away in it.

Brother and I opened the front door and waited for them. As soon as Mother saw us she called out, "Children, the Kimbroughs own a Waverly."

Brother and I went immediately to the kitchen to tell Hilda the news, and we didn't hear any further details until we were having dinner. Mother explained then, that the Waverly had her confidence not only because of the intelligent arrangement of its steering and speed controls but also because going down Michigan Avenue on the way uptown, the demonstrator, who had by then taken over the driving—another time it would not be necessary—had blinked the lights on and off as they passed the Waverly salesroom. It was just dusk.

"He told me that everyone who owns a Waverly always does that," Mother said. "I knew then that Waverly owners and Waverly makers are good friends. That signal was like a fraternity handclasp, so the machine must be dependable."

Our Waverly was delivered the next day, and all that month we went for a ride every pleasant evening. Mother had dinner moved up to six o'clock so that we could catch the sunset afterglow on the lake and over the lagoon in Jackson Park. We would rush through the meal. Brother was inclined ordinarily to dawdle over his food, but one warning from Mother that he would be left behind would set him briskly on the march again. Hilda told Brother and me she distrusted anything that came of hurrying. She said she would not care to ride in the electric until we all got more settled down. But she approved of early dinner.

Brother and I would race down the stairs ahead of Mother and Father and wait for Mother to get the Waverly out of the barn, now called the garage, insisting to her that the sun had practically set. Father waited on the sidewalk at the end of the driveway to make sure, he said, that the street was clear. I think he couldn't let go the memory of our first sortie from the driveway to the Stephens' front gate, and wanted to be certain that Mother had an unobstructed getaway, in case she should confuse her motions again.

She never did. She drove with a firm hand and a firm foot. Her footwork was of a special sort. It served as a kind of extra brake for Brother and me. He and I always sat at either end of the front seat, which was narrow and extended the width of the machine. The conventional way to use this seat was to face the driver, with both feet on the floor and one's back against the front window. But Brother and I sat facing each other, our backs against the side door windows, to allow Mother full view ahead. In this position we could not put our feet on the floor, we had to stretch them in front of us along the seat, my feet against Brother's thigh, and vice versa. In this position we had nothing to hold on to, so whenever Mother stopped suddenly, or swooped around a

corner, as she liked to do, she simultaneously put her foot
up hard against our legs to keep us from falling off sideways to the floor. The action became so involuntary with
her that once rounding a corner fast, when she was taking
for a drive old Mrs. Dyer, a neighbor, and two other ladies,
she put her foot up into Mrs. Dyer's lap and pushed hard
against her stomach. Mrs. Dyer was sitting on the front
seat in the conventional position, her back to the window,
her feet well braced on the floor.

Mother told me later what she'd done, adding that it had
made Mrs. Dyer nervous, and that when I learned to drive,
I must remember not to put my foot up.

After the first two weeks, the novelty of riding in the
Waverly wore off for Brother and me, but it was supplanted
by an exciting by-product: visits to a motion picture theater.
We never knew when these might take place, because they
happened only when the power in the electric ran down.
We charged the machine ourselves by means of an apparatus
that Father had had installed in the garage.

This apparatus gave off a crackling sound and a blue light
which disturbed the neighbors at night. One evening we
even had a visit from the police who had had a report that
our garage was haunted. After that Mother, out of consideration and over Father's protest, would run the charger
only in the daytime and in short spurts. That was why the
electric frequently ran down on an evening's drive. But
Mother found that if you let the electric rest for an hour or
two, it would in some mysterious way generate enough
power all by itself to get us home. So we would abandon
the dead car and march off to the nearest motion picture.
This was Father's idea; Mother didn't approve of motion
pictures, but she agreed to the arrangement because she felt
that to wait in any other place for two hours, or more, would

make us conspicuous. Brother and I got to see three install-
ments of *The Adventures of Kathleen* by turning off the
switch of the charging machine on days we knew the serial
was playing.

In April that year I went to Muncie, as usual, to spend
my spring vacation with my grandparents. While I was
there, Grandfather taught me to drive Grandmother's
Waverly. His method was simple, and hair-raising. He drove
me up Main Street, that had a streetcar track down the
middle of it, and explained, as he drove, every detail of the
machine. I had heard it all from the demonstrators, and
their language was easier to understand, because Grandfather was an orator. I had also been watching Mother
drive, which I told Grandfather. He was aware of that, he
said, and had therefore given only a recapitulating sum-
mary. He then stopped the electric and got out.

"Take the machine, Emily," he said to me through a window. "I have clarified your own observations on how to
conduct it. Your grandmother is waiting at the house. I
think she wishes to be taken to market. You can give her a
surprise by driving her yourself." He looked up the street
and added, "I perceive the trolley coming, but it must be
at least two blocks away. You had better turn around and
clear the tracks before it reaches you. Good-by. I have an
errand here."

I did not drive Grandmother to market. By the time I
reached the house I was bawling, though I had been helped
and encouraged by the motorman, the conductor, and most
of the passengers on the trolley. Perhaps Grandfather didn't
see the performance. At any rate, he didn't come back to
help me, and when that evening Grandmother rounded
on him, for putting me through such an ordeal he looked
amazed and wounded.

"Why, Margaret," he told her, "Emily said she wanted to learn to drive."

When I returned to Chicago at the end of vacation, I was lofty about my driving, and told Brother it was a pity he was too young to learn. Father said he considered my age equally inappropriate, but Mother told him she had worked out a plan for me that was perfectly safe, because it was only three blocks, and she had never heard of anyone's having an accident on a drive of only three blocks. I was to drive myself to and from Miss Faulkner's School, at Forty-eighth Street and Dorchester Avenue, on the two days when we had afternoon sessions. One was for basketball, the other for dancing class. Walking home alone in the late afternoon *was* dangerous, she thought. It was, however, on the three-block trip in the Waverly, that I came to grief.

I was driving home from dancing class, when, on the turn from Dorchester Avenue to Fiftieth Street, the speed lever stuck between third and fourth speeds. I jiggled it, I tried to push it ahead, to pull it back. I couldn't budge it. It was frozen, and I was rounding the corner at a clip of about twenty miles an hour, or better. I couldn't stop because I had been severely warned that in an electric, if you put on the brake while the current was on, you burned out the motor after first setting it on fire, and the motor was immediately under the driver's seat. You could tap the brake lightly for a very slight pause, but for a genuine slowing down, you had to pull the speed lever back to neutral, and then apply the brake. After that you started all over again, neutral to first, et cetera.

I only remembered about tapping the brake after I had got round the corner and settled on to four wheels again. I tapped my way around the corner at Fiftieth and Blackstone. Simultaneously, I began to ring the bell, which was a button at the end of the steering rod. I had only half a block to go before reaching our apartment. I knew I couldn't stop there, but I thought I might attract someone's attention.

The first time past brought no results, so I went on around the block, brake-tapping at the corners, though the seat beneath me was beginning to feel hot. I had also gathered speed, so I approached the apartment on the second try at a mileage per hour that I had experienced before only on a Flexible Flyer. But I was ready with my message in flight, in case there was anyone to receive it. At the corner I stopped ringing the bell, braced my knee against the steering rod to hold a steady course, leaned out the window, my hands cupped around my mouth, and roared over and over, "Mother, come help! Mother, help! *Mother!*"

I was afraid that people in the apartments would be the only ones to hear me and have to relay the news to Mother, but miraculously it was Hilda who heard and recognized my voice and the bell of our electric. I saw her come out on the porch my next time round the block. But she shook her finger crossly as I flashed by, and yelled after me, "Shame on you."

Part way around the block I was confused by this; then I guessed she had thought I was showing off how I could drive no-handed, and wouldn't on any account let Mother see. But the next time past, I saw Mother beside Hilda on the porch. "Come in this minute," she called down very loud and she repeated it. This prevented her from hearing what I was saying. Going around the corner, I burst into tears. I had been sure that once I got Mother's attention, she would know what was wrong and what to do.

That lap was the most dangerous of all the trips around the block. The noise of my bell made several people who

She made it, swinging onto the running board.

were crossing the street jump into the air and then scurry to the sidewalk. They were angry, too, because an electric didn't make any noise, so the first warning they had was the bell. Motorcars and horse-drawn delivery wagons should have impeded me, but I zigzagged around all of them. When I rounded on to Blackstone Avenue again, Mother had guessed that I couldn't stop. She was standing in the middle of the street. A number of people from our building were on their porches, watching. She pantomimed by bending her knees and swinging her arms that she was going to jump onto my runningboard. As I reached her, I tapped the brake so hard that the motor sizzled under me. She made it, swinging on to the runningboard on the side opposite me, and held on by thrusting her arm through the window, which fortunately was open. She crouched to talk to me through the window. "You're doing nicely," she said. "What's the matter? Stop crying."

"The speed lever's stuck." I jiggled it to show her, and I stopped crying. When she had satisfied herself that the lever *was* stuck, she straightened up, looked over the top, and shouted, first to people in our way, then equally loud but sticking her face suddenly through the window, to me.

"Out of our way, little boy. . . . We could keep on driving 'til the power dies. . . . Look out, *please*, we're out of control. . . . Not around and around like this, Emily, we'll be dizzy. . . . Keep *back*, please. . . . But in a straight line we might be in Gary before we stop. Ring the bell louder. . . . Don't be a fool (this to a man on the curb who called something to us), we're not doing this on pur. . . ." We had shot past him by this time and were in our own street again, which was quieter. It gave Mother time to think. She leaned reflectively over the window ledge.

"I *will* not pass all those people again," she said. "They

don't seem to understand what we're doing. They make me feel like a fool."

"Where do you want me to go?" I asked her. She had an inspiration. "Go across Fifty-first Street," she directed, "and up Lake Park. There's a nice garage somewhere along that block. Mrs. Dyer told me. Very courteous, she said. We can ask which it is."

We crossed Fifty-first Street, turned left, and right on Lake Park Avenue. There seemed to be several garages on each side of the street.

"Ring the bell again," Mother told me, "but stop when someone comes out so I can talk to him."

I rang steadily, but no one came. So I drove once around *that* block. At the second round, Mother changed the plan of approach. "Don't ring," she ordered, "shout 'ahoy' with me. That's more unusual. It may bring someone."

It did. It brought two or three men out of almost every garage on the run.

Mother said, "Quiet, Emily," and straightened to her full height. "Are you Mrs. Dyer's garage," she called as we whirled by. No one answered.

"I surprised them, I think," Mother said as we went around the block again. "You have to present ideas slowly to people like that. They work with their hands. It makes them deliberate. And yet surgeons, they tell me, respond quickly to a crisis. Broader preliminary education probably."

We turned into Lake Park for the third time. Some of the men who had come out at our shouts were still in front of the garages. Mother addressed them, leaning out from the running board, her one arm upraised.

"My daughter," she said rapidly but clear and loud, "my daughter has had an accident. Not really an accident. She only drives three blocks. To Miss Faulkner's School . . . for basketball. I am Mrs. H. C. Kimbrough, 5019 Blackstone Avenue." We passed the last garage . . . "and dancing, on Wednesdays," she called back.

We had reached the corner. Mother didn't talk as we made the next circuit, but at Fifty-first and Lake Park she got ready again. This time I saw only one man in the whole block. He was young and thin and dirty. He slouched over to the curb as we rushed toward him and dropped into the gutter a cigarette he'd been smoking. He was on my side of the machine. I don't think Mother even saw him. She called down to me, "Ring again, Emily, and shout. We'll have to start all over again."

I was watching the young man. He stepped into the street and put up his hand, palm toward me, like a traffic police-man. I tapped the brake as hard as I dared. He stepped with no particular effort on the running board next me. I stopped tapping and the Waverly shot forward again. He held the sill of my window in one hand, leaned inside, reached down beside me and pulled out the key that connected the cur-rent. The machine slowed down. I put on the brake hard, and we stopped.

Mother apparently didn't realize at once that we had stopped. Her face appeared in the window, and she seemed about to speak to me when she saw the face of the man in the opposite window. She spoke to him instead.

"Oh," she said, "I'm glad to see you. Are you Mrs. Dyer's garage?"

"No, ma'am," he said finally, "I don't think so." He looked at me, and pointed to the speed lever. "That hap-pens every once in a while," he said. "All you got to do is disconnect the current. People never seem to think of it. They don't think quick, I guess."

17. Graduation

WHEN I GRADUATED FROM MISS FAULKNER'S SCHOOL WE had lived in Chicago five years. I had learned a good many things not included in the curriculum of a college preparatory course. I had mastered the curtsy and not long after accomplishing that feat had been told I was too old to do it any more. I stood up automatically when an older person came into the room, but I had learned other things less tangible than those, about the social customs of people who lived in cities.

When I talked about these to Mother, I found them difficult to explain. They had something to do with the approach of well-mannered people to one another.

"For example," I said to Mother, "I think in towns like Muncie we're more direct. For instance, you'd say to your friend, Mrs. Ball, 'Frances, Hal and I have a chance to go to Chicago for a couple of days. Could you take Emily?'

"And Mrs. Ball would say, yes, she'd be delighted, or no, it wouldn't be convenient, and suggest that you try Grace Rich. But in Chicago, though you've made awfully good friends, I don't suppose you'd dream of doing such a thing. If you *could* conceive of doing it, I'm sure you'd say something like, 'I have the most tremendous favor to ask of you, and I can only do it if you'll promise to be perfectly frank in your answer. It's an emergency or I shouldn't even dream of suggesting it, but do you think by any possibility that you could,' et cetera.

"And then, if your friend did say she'd be delighted, you'd go on protesting, asking was she absolutely sure, and you didn't believe she was really being frank, until you finally arrived at a subtle understanding that satisfied you both."

Mother agreed that the two conversations would be somewhat as I'd given them.

I reminded her that when she had asked Mrs. Huey if Ruth could go with us to *The Ring* and *Parsifal*, given by the Chicago Opera Company on five successive Sundays, the telephone conversation between them had lasted half an hour or more: Mother protesting that we really did want her very much, and Mrs. Huey that it would be inconvenient, until they had finally got around to agreeing that Ruth could go with us and spend the night with me because it would be so late when we returned.

"All that roundabout palavering," I added, "like mandarins bowing at each other, seems to be part of what sophistication means. It's a kind of special jargon. And what's more," I added, "you have to know when to use it."

I had learned that I had to be very careful about carrying back the customs and the jargon to Muncie. The first time on a return visit there that I had stood up when Grandmother entered the room, she had asked me where I was going. She was a little annoyed, perhaps because I was lofty about it, when I explained what I was doing. The first time I curtsied to a neighbor come in to call, both the neighbor and my grandmother thought I had dropped something and was stooping to pick it up. I explained the custom, but after the caller had gone, Grandmother asked me not to do it again. She said it looked to her too much like the goings-on in a Catholic Church. If I said "lunch and dinner" there, I was affected. If I used that exaggerated, and what I called secret, jargon of sophisticated politeness, I was putting on airs. If I mentioned plays, operas, or concerts I had attended, I was showing off. Other people from Muncie saw those things, too, but always on a trip. For me to refer to weekly concerts, or the season of opera, was therefore irritating.

Grandmother had been relieved to know that I had never been in a beauty parlor. When I asserted that I was longing to patronize one, she told me she was sorry to hear it. I explained my reason. Mrs. Breen came on Saturday mornings to wash my hair and Mother's. Mrs. Breen was a lady in our neighborhood, I said, who lost her husband and was left without any money. She was too genteel and too untrained to go into any business, so Mother had had the idea of getting her to wash the hair of people in the neighborhood whom she knew, or at least knew by sight. This had proved satisfactory to her but not to me, because, though she was thorough in her shampoos, she was not deft, and consistently filled my eyes and ears with soap. Grandmother's answer, when I had explained this to her, was, "A little soap never hurt anyone. But if you go lolling back in a beauty parlor, not even having to bend over a basin, pretty soon you won't be able to lift a finger to anything."

On that same visit, someone had asked, "Since when have you taken to saying, 'trolley' and 'block' instead of 'streetcar' and 'square'?"

And yet in Chicago I was still the Hoosier hayseed. My Faulkner schoolmates were closer to me than my friends in Muncie, but the Chicago ones laughed frequently at my unconscious insertion into a conversation of what they called, "Hoosier talk." I didn't mind. I loved my friends, I loved Chicago. I didn't want to live in Muncie again.

But I said to Mother one night that I sometimes wondered if I would ever feel that I belonged anywhere. Mother's answer was that I probably wouldn't.

"We were pulled up by the roots and have never been put down firm again. Still, I don't know that that's a bad thing," she added. "Attachment to things or places is very confining."

A month before our graduation Bower and I went in town to the Fine Arts Building and took our Bryn Mawr entrance examinations. We were the only candidates. We sat in a large room, watched over by two proctors in cap and gown. The examinations were held on three successive days. Mrs. Kelly and Mother went with us, and waited outside the "torture room" as we called it. They took us to lunch each day, but Bower and I were too miserable to eat. We brought with us the paper of that morning's examination and went over it with our mothers, question by question, trying to estimate our chances of passing.

Bower pinned her hopes on Mathematics. That subject was so very easy for her she was in the habit of saving time by having her mother read aloud the English assignment, while she did her Algebra or Geometry. Not only were her Mathematics papers consistently perfect, but her absorption of the English assignment was thoroughly satisfactory. I saw no faint possibility of my passing Mathematics, because, though I had memorized almost the whole of the Algebra and Geometry textbooks, I had never understood nor been able to solve a problem not included there. English was to be my salvation. My themes were almost always read aloud either at assembly or to my class, and I was a heavy

No one could help noticing Perk.

contributor to the school publication. We were both scared that Latin and Greek might be tricky, and I said over and over that if they asked for maps in Ancient History, I was done for.

The senior parties began immediately after spring vacation, but Bower and I were not allowed to go to any of them until our Bryn Mawr entrance examinations were over. Once these were finished, we were in a whirl of entertainment.

Each senior chose from the lower classes two girls to be her attendants at commencement: one an usher, the other a flower-girl. The attendants gave parties for their seniors, and every senior had a party for the other seniors and the attendants.

Mother bought for me a book bound in pale blue suede with gold lettering across the cover that read, *The Girl Graduate—Her Own Book.* I wrote down the plays to which we went. *Sherlock Holmes, Marie Odille, The Chief, It Pays to Advertise, Bunker Bean, Watch Your Step, Chin Chin* and *Young America.* On another page I listed my presents as they arrived: gold mesh bag from Grandmother Wiles, a cameo necklace from a great-uncle and aunt, camisole and bloomers from Mrs. Breen. I regretted all the harsh things I had said about the way she washed my hair. She had made the camisole and bloomers herself, the first silk underwear I had ever owned. A yellow bedroom thermos bottle, a silver vanity bag, a yellow jar of Ruskin pottery, a yellow hatpin holder—yellow was my favorite color—a book of Kashmir with colored illustrations, a pair of arts-and-crafts lingerie clasps, a pair of silk stockings, my first, a powder-puff holder, a small fan, were on the list.

Other pages were reserved for the signature and an appropriate sentiment from each of my teachers, and the members of my class.

The night before graduation was the senior dance. I invited Perk Hart. He was a freshman at Yale now, home for summer vacation just in time for the party. Mine was by far the most distinguished partner. The only other boys we knew were those with whom we danced at Miss Hinman's class in Helena Meinrath's ballroom, to which I had gone for two years. None of those boys were in college yet, let alone Yale.

Because I was the head of Student Government I was to lead the grand march. Bower, as secretary and treasurer, would come with her partner immediately behind us. I explained this to Mother as she helped me dress.

"No one," I added, "can help noticing Perk."

The one who noticed him particularly was Marguerite Fellows, and he noticed her simultaneously. He asked to be introduced to her, and as of that moment forgot about me except when I reminded him. Some of the dances that he forgot I sat out beside Miss Faulkner; others I danced with Marguerite's leftover. I didn't go near Mother, who was one of the chaperones, because I didn't want her to talk to me about it. But on the way home in the electric, with Mother there, I asked Perk if he thought he had fallen in love with Marguerite. No one in my class had fallen in love; we even thought talking about it was silly. But watching Marguerite and Perk had given me a funny feeling.

Perk stumbled around a little, but finally said, yes, he guessed he had.

When we'd left him at his apartment, Mother said on the way home that I shouldn't have asked him such a thing, especially in front of her. She added that I needn't tell her if I didn't want to, but she hoped I wasn't upset and wounded by the news.

I thought about this after I had gone to bed and decided that I wasn't very upset, but I was surprised, and indignant. I made up my mind before I went to sleep, however, that I would bring home on my first vacation from Bryn Mawr, three or four, possibly half a dozen, assorted beaus, from Yale, Harvard and Princeton.

Grandmother and Grandfather arrived the next morning from Muncie and Grandmother Wiles from Indianapolis. With the commencement scheduled at eight o'clock in the evening, they would have a full day to rest and make ready for the occasion. They looked at all my presents and at the flowers that had begun to arrive. They admired my graduation dress I brought out for their inspection. Even Brother was impressed by the flowers and brought some of his friends up to take a look at them. I chased them out, however, lest they start some kind of a roughhouse in the living room where the bouquets were on display.

I was too excited to eat lunch, but I was sitting at the table with the family when Hilda brought in the noon mail. In it was a letter to me from Bryn Mawr College. My hands began to shake, and I said, "It's from Bryn Mawr."

Everyone stopped talking and watched me while I opened it. I had passed Latin, Greek and Ancient History, the communication read, and I had failed Mathematics and English. I could not come to college in the fall, but I could repeat the examinations the following year.

Sometime in the afternoon Mrs. Kelly telephoned to say that Bower wanted me to know she had passed her English, Latin and Greek, but had failed in Mathematics, and would have to repeat the examination the following year. Bower herself, Mrs. Kelly told Mother, was unable to speak on the telephone. She had been crying steadily since the news had arrived in the mail at noon.

I had been weeping, too, violently, bitterly, with such anguish as I had never before known, begging my family to leave me alone in my room (Grandfather was announcing his intention of taking the next train to Philadelphia and speaking personally with the President of Bryn Mawr) saying over and over to Mother who sat beside me as I lay on my bed I could not go through the graduation that night. It was a farce. I was not graduating. I was a failure.

Finally, at some time I dropped off to sleep. When I woke, Mother was not in the room, but there was a note in her handwriting on the chair where she had sat. I read it, and in part it said,

So let's up with our shields again until we are brought back, finally, on them. And remember, we all stumble, every one of us. That's why it's a comfort to go hand in hand. So don't forget that father's hand is on one side of you, and mother's on the other. And let's start off again: one, two; one, two. . . .